John Trollope
Record Breaker

John Trollope
Record Breaker

by Peter Matthews

breedon **books**
PUBLISHING

First published in Great Britain in 2006 by
The Breedon Books Publishing Company Limited
Breedon House, 3 The Parker Centre, Derby, DE21 4SZ.

ISBN 1 85983 495 7

Printed and bound by Cromwell Press, Trowbridge, Wiltshire.

CONTENTS

DEDICATION

To my wonderful wife Jeanie,
with love and thanks.

ACKNOWLEDGEMENTS

Any book, regardless of whose name appears on the front cover, is a team effort. My thanks go to all who have supported me over the past few months.

Special thanks are due to John for his hospitality and patience during the many sessions at his home, and to Maureen for her unfailing good humour whenever I phoned up to ask yet another question of either her or John. Thanks also to John's children, Sara and Paul, for their time and insights, and also to those who spoke to me about John's career in football, most notably Frank Burrows, Peter Downsborough, Lou Macari and Don Rogers.

The original idea for this book came from an introduction to John via Podge Rogers, who continued to support me during the writing of this book with his cheery and encouraging phone calls. Mike Judd, as for my previous book on Don Rogers, was also a great source of support, as were my family, particularly my father, Alan, a long-suffering Swindon Town season-ticket holder.

My thanks also to all at Breedon, particularly Steve Caron and Susan Last, for their support.

JOHN TROLLOPE
INTRODUCTION

Left-back. The very words bring to mind the old schoolboy jokes about a player's best position being left back in the changing room. It's not the most sought after position on the pitch, indeed in some ways it might be the least.

Need convincing? How many famous left-backs can you name? Roberto Carlos, Stuart Pearce, Ashley Cole? How many others? Even go back to 1966, and English football's greatest day – the winning of the World Cup. Who was the left-back on that day at Wembley against Germany? George Cohen? No, he was right-back. Ah yes, that's him, Ray Wilson – didn't he go on and become an undertaker – I suppose that's a reasonable career choice for a left-back – an unglamorous choice from someone who played in an unglamorous position.

Indeed, more recently left-backs have tended to be more famous for their tough-tackling and, er, off-pitch reputations. Julian Dicks, once of West Ham, Mark Dennis, once of Southampton and Birmingham, and Pat Van Den Hauwe, once of Everton and Spurs, would fall into this category – all 'hard men'. Even Stuart Pearce, for all his football talent, was known universally as 'Psycho' during his playing career.

However, this is a biography of a left-back. Moreover, this left-back never played international football; in truth he was never remotely considered for selection. His playing career spanned three decades, yet only seven seasons were spent out of the bottom two

Divisions of English football; he never played at the top level. He did play in, and win, a Cup Final at Wembley, although he nearly missed that because of injury. Off the pitch he led a happy and stable family life, and his name won't be found in any accounts of misbehaving footballers. Yet John Trollope is worthy of a biography because he holds a football record, which, in this day of Bosmans, agents and short-term thinking, is unlikely to ever be broken – the most League games for one football club.

True, players have played more games – both Peter Shilton and Tony Ford have played more than 1,000 competitive first-class games of football, and, deservedly, both have received great accolades for their efforts. Both players, though, played for eight League clubs. But when John Trollope played for Swindon at home to Carlisle United on 18 October 1980, he passed the previous record of 764 League games played for one club, held by Jimmy Dickinson, 'Gentleman Jim', from Portsmouth. But for an injury during Swindon's annus mirabilis, 1968–69, he would surely have also beaten Tranmere Rovers' Harold Bell's record for the most consecutive League games – the broken arm Trollope suffered at Hartlepool left him on a run of 368 games, less than a season's worth of games behind Bell's record of 401 consecutive games.

In all, Trollope played over 880 first-team competitive games for Swindon Town, his only club. For his loyalty and commitment to the club, he was awarded not only a PFA Merit Award but also an MBE. Not bad for a left-back!

In a sense, this is a book that has three different stories within its pages. Firstly, this is John Trollope's story, written with his full co-operation and also the full support of his family, including his son, Paul, a professional footballer himself. His family have their say on John's career at the end of the book. Throughout the story, one is struck by the constant loyalty shown by John towards his club through good and also many bad times. As we shall see, in the end that loyalty was not reciprocated – the story of John's parting with the club, told here from John's point of view for the first time, is a very sad one and one that reflects poorly on the club.

Secondly, this is a post-war history of Swindon Town Football Club. John's involvement with the club, as supporter, player, manager and coach, spanned five decades. He was involved with the club during seven promotion seasons (including the season when he was sacked by the club and the season when promotion was won on the pitch, only to be lost off it) and five relegation seasons. He played for the club in a Wembley Cup Final and was involved, when on the backroom staff, in two successful Wembley Play-off Finals, as well as two League Cup semi-finals. His recollections span the most dramatic period in the Club's history, and the story includes his views on the various managers with whom he was involved at the County Ground – from Bert Head to Steve McMahon.

Thirdly, this is a story of the way football used to be. As the tale unfolds, starting in the 1950s, we can see the way the game has changed down the years. John is too astute an observer of the game to believe that 'everything was better in my day', and this is a balanced account of the good and bad changes in the game over his years in football. However, in his accounts of how things used to be in terms of training, contracts, matchday routines and summer jobs, we can sense a different, less complicated age, and there is surely some learning there for the frenetic, over commercialised, modern game.

Above all, this is a very human story – the story of how a shy boy from Wroughton became a record breaker.

EARLY DAYS

Local boy, local man. The story of John Trollope is one of somebody who has lived all his life within 10 miles of the town where he made his name – Swindon.

It all started on 14 June 1943 when John was born in Wroughton, back then a village just outside Swindon. Nowadays, as Swindon has expanded over the years, Wroughton is virtually indistinguishable from the urban sprawl and succession of modern housing estates that make up the former railway town. Norman John Trollope, as he was christened (in due deference to his father, Norman), was the youngest of five siblings, only just, mind, as he was one of twins, joining the world fractionally after his twin-sister Jean. Besides Jean, he has two other sisters, Mary and Margaret, and a brother, Bill.

'I was born in North Wroughton, which is the Swindon side of Wroughton, and brought up in an old terraced house there. My dad worked in the railways, as of course so many people did back then, in the stores, and my mum, Mary, who is still alive at 93 and living very close to where we were brought up, looked after us all.

I went to school at Wroughton, firstly to the junior school and then to the Secondary Modern – I didn't get into grammar school, and I remember that I had a very happy childhood really – lots of time playing outside – we didn't have that much in the way of toys because they were quite hard years, immediately after the war.'

John, like many other boys of that era, spent his time playing endless games of football. It was a very different era then in terms of what children wanted and were allowed to do.

'Football was a very popular sport with everybody in those days.

I started off playing in the road and we used to have to stop when there was a shout of "car coming", then we played in the field opposite where I lived and then at the local recreation ground, "The Rec" or Weir Field as it was called, playing 20-a-side with the coats down for goalposts. We played against much older boys, which was good preparation for later – everybody just mixed in.

I was told that I had a little bit extra to some of the boys, but I would never say I was outstanding – I just had good basics, which developed through playing so much in the village and then at junior and senior school. I also spent a lot of time kicking a ball against a garage at the back of our house with my friends, and that helped me get my technique right.

We never played in any minor leagues, like they do today; the games I played in were either schools games, or Cub Scout games, where we used to play against other packs. The only other games we played in were games we organised ourselves, where we used to go over on our bikes and play villages like Bishopston and Wanborough. They were good fun, again not properly organised games but a good kickabout. It wouldn't happen now – for one thing, I don't think in your early teens you'd cycle by yourself. Sometimes one of the dads would put posts up, but normally it would be jumpers.'

It is evident that John enjoyed a happy and contented childhood, part of which came from a settled family life and part from a circle of friends that he developed, one of whom remains one of John's closest friends over 50 years on.

'I made some very good friends in Wroughton in the early days. One of them is Brian Hacker, who I went to school with and have been mates with ever since. Whenever I have had any problems during my career, Brian has always been there to offer support and advice, along with his wife, Andrea, and family.'

John's love of football was clear, even at this early age. During the writing of this book, his mother reminded him that he was instrumental in setting up the football team at Wroughton Junior School – at the age of 10!

While football dominated John's early years, there was one other competing hobby:

'I did play in the Wroughton Silver Band for a time – flugelhorn – which was good fun. Unfortunately, once I started playing for Swindon Boys the training sessions began clashing with band practise and football took over. I suppose I must have stopped playing in the band when I was fourteen or fifteen.'

It was around this time that John was first exposed to the club that he would loyally serve for nearly 40 years.

'I started out watching Wroughton, but then as I got older, during the mid 1950s, we used to go by bus to the County Ground to watch Swindon. I remember seeing all the players of that era: George Hunt, George Hudson, Sammy Burton and Maurice Owen. I was particularly struck by Maurice Owen, he was a great header of the ball despite not being very tall. It was a big thing for me to make my debut with Maurice, who of course by then was a centre-half – he had been a bit of a hero to me when I was growing up.'

This was to be a golden era for school football in the town of Swindon. While playing for Wroughton, John would play against a number of boys who would be his professional football colleagues.

'We played all the schools in Swindon, so I played against people like Terry Wollen and Ernie Hunt, who played for their schools. In those days I was a right-half not a left-back.'

'Good, but not outstanding', as John describes himself, seems an odd thing to say about someone who would have such a long and distinguished career, but the facts would seem to bear that out. Partly because of the fact that there were so many good players in the Swindon area of his age at that time, and partly because he may have been a 'late developer', he failed to make the under-14 Swindon Boys side. It wasn't until he got into the under-15 side that he first joined forces with people with whom he was to progress all the way to the Football League.

'I don't know why I didn't get into the under-14s really. I think part of it may have been that, although it sounds stupid to say it now, Wroughton was a bit 'out in the sticks' and so wasn't as fashionable as some of the town-centre schools. You had to be recommended by your schoolteacher and perhaps his views weren't taken as seriously as others.

That Swindon Boys side was superb – Roger Smart, Ernie Hunt, Wilf Shergold, Terry Wollen and all played, and we all went on to play professionally for Swindon. I think, in fairness, they were a bit ahead of me at that stage as footballers – perhaps they were a bit more streetwise as townies than us country boys!

The year I got in, the under-15s got through to the English Schools' Shield quarter-finals – we lost to a team in London, Dagenham I think it was, Terry Venables played for them. I was just a squad player in the first part of the season, but then I forced my way into the side for the second half of the season, and for me the big thing was that we used to play on the County Ground pitch for the big games on Saturday mornings, games in the Schools' Shield and the Cabot Cup, which was a Cup for teams in the area, although the area must have been quite big because we played West Bromwich, I recall.'

One thing that was different for the youngster was exposure to 'proper' coaching. Wroughton teachers, including, John says, the female ones, had all taken the teams and done what they could, but now, with the cream of Swindon's schoolboys, there was some focused coaching

'The two people who took Swindon Boys were Fred Coleman and Bill Gleed, who were both schoolteachers. Fred, in particular, was a big influence. You listened to what he had to say and tried to act on it, especially on the right way to play the game.

I don't think I suffered at all from not having formal coaching until I was fourteen and a half, in fact, I just wonder if there is something we can learn from today with all the youngsters being coached, some might say over coached, from such a young age. My view is that you should just be allowed to play and enjoy it when you are a youngster. There again, perhaps I would have been a better player if I had been coached – we'll never know.

The main thing I needed to work on at that age was beating players. I could always pass, and I was a good runner, but I needed some help in beating people. Some of the things that they practise now in terms of how to beat people, like the Cruyff turn (which of course didn't exist then), would have been very helpful. In my day the coaches worked on what you could do, they didn't focus on what you couldn't do. Looking back, it might have been better if they'd worked on our faults as well. I might have become more comfortable on the ball then.'

Despite this progress on the football field, John, at this stage, wasn't thinking of a career in football, and although he could have left school in the summer of 1958, at the age of 15, he decided to stay on and do another year.

'I just wanted to stay on and do something extra really. I did a book-keeping course, a sort of commercial conversion year in some ways – maths was my strong subject. So I didn't leave school until I was 16, and then I went and worked in the accounts department of a company called Rentaset in Rodbourne, which, as its name implies, was a TV rental company.'

That extra year at school didn't hold back his football though, and he carried on playing representative football with the contemporaries. The difference was that Swindon Boys had now become Swindon Town.

'What used to happen was that virtually all the Swindon Boys side used to be signed on by Swindon Town, some on the groundstaff and others on non-contract forms. We then used to play in the Borough League as under-16-and-a-half players, against sides like Pinehurst, Rodbourne and Ferndale. They were good competitive games because nearly every boy in the town wanted to play football.

I was still right-half at this stage – I could get up and down the pitch, and I was a good passer of the ball. Because I was still at school, I was playing in that team with others who were already on the groundstaff.'

The youngster had impressed at schoolboy level, but not sufficiently to be offered a contract at Swindon Town on the groundstaff when aged 16,

unlike some of his contemporaries who had been taken on, hence his brief spell at Rentaset.

'I don't think they thought I was quite good enough to make it. I was by no means the star player, and I was still developing as a player. They could afford to see how I would progress as a non-contract player.

I played for the second youth team, and it was only when I got picked for the "A" team that they decided to take me on full-time. Ellis Stuttard came out and saw my mum and dad and said they wanted me to join the groundstaff. Like many parents, I think mum and dad had their reservations – they wanted me to have a "proper" job. However, they saw it was a real chance for me, and they thought I could always go back into book-keeping if it didn't work out, so I signed.

When I joined, many of the people I went on and played with were already there: Mike Summerbee, Roger Smart, Ernie Hunt and Terry Wollen had been taken on over the summer. You've got to remember that Swindon were fielding lots of teams back then, the first team, the reserves, two "A" teams and two youth teams, with all the sides playing on a Saturday.'

It was a golden era for Swindon youth football. As we shall see, not only were four of John's teammates from Swindon Boys to play with him in the first team but there were other previous graduates of Swindon Boys who also made the grade: Keith Morgan, Bobby Woodruff and Cliff Jackson to name but three. Don Rogers and Mike Summerbee may have played their school football outside Swindon, but both came through the youth team at Swindon to make their first-team debuts for the club. It begs the obvious question: 'why?'

'I wish I could tell you why it happened because then I could have done the same thing when I was youth-team boss! Perhaps it was luck, or perhaps it was the era we were born in. If you look at it, there were a huge number of professional footballers born towards the end of the war, for example a lot of the great Leeds team of the Billy Bremner era were born at that time as well.

Perhaps we were just affected by being raised in the years immediately after the war, I don't know.'

So in October 1959 John joined the club with whom he made his name. Initially, he played in the 'A' teams. Swindon, as mentioned, ran two 'A' teams, one of which played in the Wiltshire Premier League and one in the Hellenic Premier League. Both were hard Leagues to learn football in.

'We got some real kickings because we were a bunch of kids up against men, all of whom wanted to say they'd beaten Swindon Town. Nowadays, coaches would be very against playing 16-year-olds against men, unless you were a Rooney, because of the physical demands on your body. There were a sprinkling of older players – I remember we played at Calne once and Bronco Layne played and got sent off! But mainly it was youngsters.'

Despite the challenges on the pitch, John soon settled into the life of a professional footballer, which, as today, contained its share of practical jokes.

'We used to get changed in the old cricket pavilion, by the main stand. Anyway, all the locally-born players used to get changed in the away dressing room in the pavilion, so you had players like Maurice Owen, Sammy Burton and George Hudson from the older pros, along with people like Ernie, Terry, Cliff Jackson, Bobby Woodruff, Mike Summerbee and Keith Morgan, who were local youngsters. It was new, but it was helped by the fact that I'd played with so many of the players through Swindon Boys and youth teams.

Anyway, on one of my first days I went in and Sammy Burton came over to me and said "don't worry son, I'll look after you – come and change here". So I'm changing next to him and big George Hudson, who was a massive fellow, he probably wouldn't play professional football now because he was so big, came in, and of course Sam has set me up and I'm using his peg. Sam saw I was a bit shy and quiet, probably a bit timid really, so he was always ready to set me up.

But it was a great time: people like Sam, George and Maurice

Owen really enjoyed being professional footballers, and they were always playing practical jokes, particularly Maurice and Sam. Maurice would put the ammunition in and Sam used to fire it. We used to have this old guy called Jim Waller who used to bring the tea in, and he carried it in a big, enamel jug. I lost count of the number of times that Sam used to slip a bar of soap in the jug as Jim went past and then get the players to complain about the taste of the tea.

Sam also used to do things like nailing shoes to the floor, cutting off the toes of your socks – practical jokes like that – you'd always go back into the dressing room wondering what he'd done. Then, over time, Ernie Hunt got involved as well, he was like Sam and Maurice's apprentice!'

Competition for places was fierce. There were around 40 players on the staff – a minimum of three people for each position. For the right-half position it was tough. Former Swindon schoolboy Keith Morgan was the first-team incumbent, who was slightly older than John. Fate, though, was to smile upon John, and it was to be a change in position that got him started on the route to eventual first-team football.

'There was a practise game on the County Ground, and they were light of a left-back. I wasn't supposed to be playing, but Bert Head saw me and said "on you go son, you're playing left-back". I don't know why he chose me. I think I was one of the only ones left. Anyway, it was real luck because, from then, I was in the first team in about nine months. This was not long after joining the ground-staff.

To begin with it was very strange because you tried to get the ball round on to your right foot. My left foot was reasonable, but I wasn't confident with it early on. But by the end of my career I was more accurate with my left foot than my right from set pieces, and I was nearly as good on my left foot as I was with my right in open play.'

It was to be a critical move. By the turn of the year, and the beginning of a new decade, the 16-year-old was in the reserve team; he was to play less than 15 games for them before making his first-team debut.

FIRST-TEAM DEBUT... AND A PROMOTION

John signed professional terms on his 17th birthday, in the summer of 1960. His first contract was £10 a week in the winter (a 100% pay rise from the £5 he was on previously) and £7 in the summer. Bonuses were set at £4 for a win and £2 for a draw– an important part of any players' take-home pay back then. With basic salaries for players being much lower, the importance of bonuses (or 'performance-related pay' as papers today would call it) was much greater, and perhaps it made players hungrier.

After two seasons of low, mid-table finishes (15th and 16th), Bert Head decided to accelerate his policy of blooding talented young players. Much to John's surprise, he would be the next beneficiary.

'The regular left-back was Walter Bingley, who was a good, solid player. I was expecting to spend the season playing in the reserves, after all I'd barely had any second-team football and was still learning how to play left-back.

What happened, though, was that we used to play a public practise match, Reds versus Blues or Probables versus Possibles, and the Possibles, who I, and some of the other youngsters, were playing for, beat what was supposed to be the first team by something like 7–2, and Bert Head decided to put Terry Wollen and I in the first team, really on the strength of that game.

I didn't know I was playing until the Friday when the team sheet went up. The teams always got put up the day before the game. Bert hadn't said anything about it to me, although clearly the result of the trial match had reverberated around the club. I was very nervous the night before the game, you've got to remember that I'd barely played any reserve-team games at all. Most people knew that Mike Summerbee and Ernie Hunt would make it, and Terry Wollen, too, to a certain degree, but I'd had a very rapid rise from playing right-half in the "A" team to first-team left-back in under a year. I'd matured very quickly as a player from the ages of 16 to 17 really.'

And so, on 20 August 1960, aged just 17 years and 68 days, John made his first-team debut at home to Halifax Town in a game that finished 1–1, Ernie Hunt scoring for Swindon from the penalty spot.

'I can't remember much about the game. I would know we drew without having to look the result up, but apart from feeling very nervous on the day I can't recall much about the day.'

John wasn't the only youngster blooded that day. The other full-back was Terry Wollen, also aged 17, but even younger than John, as his 17th birthday had been in July, rather than June. Wollen, whose career was tragically cut short by injury, was to be, like John, a regular during that first season.

'Terry was a really good player – a more naturally-talented player than me. Of course, I knew him well through Swindon schoolboys and then playing with him through Swindon Town youths. It was a real tragedy that he never recovered from his broken leg because I think he had the ability to follow some of the others to the top.'

John joined a team that was becoming known throughout the game as 'Bert's Babes', as not only were the full-backs youngsters but players like Cliff Jackson, Bobby Woodruff, Mike Summerbee, Keith Morgan and Ernie Hunt were all regulars that season and were all under 21. It helped the young left-back settle in quickly.

'If you look back on it, the situation was remarkable. In the team I made my debut in, five of us, Cliff, Ernie, Bobby, Terry and I, had all played for Swindon Schoolboys. It's incredible that over a period of three years the schoolboys side had produced so many good players. Then Keith and Mike had come through the youth team, even though they had started in places other than Swindon, so we had seven of the team who were very much "home-grown".'

Playing in the first team meant that John had his closest involvement to date with the manager, the legendary Bert Head. Although John had tended to train with the first team as he moved into reserve-team football, much of the training was done by Ellis Stuttard, so this exposure to Bert Head was a new experience.

'Bert was a very disciplined person. When we were on the groundstaff he used to call us in and say "let's have a look at your shoes" or "let's have a look at your hands". If you tried to do that today you'd be laughed out of court. He was a very strong man – in fact some of the stuff he did you might call bullying now. I'm not sure we saw it as bullying, we just saw him as a hard man who had very strong standards and principles. The good thing about him, though, was that he did want you to play football, and he was prepared to blood people very early – he was definitely taking a chance on the likes of Terry and me, but he had the courage to bring us in to replace good, experienced professionals like Walt Bingley and John Higgins. Not only that, but once he put young players in they stayed in and were given time to get used to playing League football.'

Despite the exuberance of the youngsters and the experience of players like goalkeeper Sam Burton and centre-half Maurice Owen, the team was inconsistent. They started well, with an unbeaten run of seven games, and finished well, with a run of eight games unbeaten, but in the middle of the season there was a long, barren run of only one win in 16 games. The team ended up in a familiar position, 16th.

John's memories of the season, other than a 1–1 draw at Bristol City, which 'locals said was one of the best games ever down there', focus mainly on the Cups.

'I don't remember much about individual games in that first season, apart from a League Cup game against Shrewsbury and an FA Cup tie at Bath. Cup games often seem more memorable somehow [presumably inevitably if you play 770 League games].

Against Shrewsbury, it was the first season of the League Cup and we lost at home in a second replay. The reason why I remember it was the pitch for the game we lost, it was terrible. They were going to abandon the game but Bert Head said "just get on with it". We were all young, of course, and the pitch was so muddy that it just sapped your strength, and they were older and stronger than us. I can remember that Sam Burton could hardly kick the ball out of the penalty area.

The Bath game was absolutely crazy. We'd been lucky in the first game. We'd been two down at half time at Swindon, and I seem to remember that Sam let one through his legs, which wouldn't have gone down well. Then, for the replay, Sam was injured, and a lad called Crook was brought in as goalkeeper for his first game for Swindon – he was a short, squat fellow from the North-East. Anyway, he was a big tea-drinker, and I can remember Bert Head having a real go at him for drinking too much tea at half time because he thought it had affected his performance! It was a great Cup tie, Bronco Layne scored four goals and we won 6–4.

For John, though, it had been an excellent season. He had missed just two games, having played in all of the first 36 games before missing two games through a stomach muscle strain at Easter 1961. At the time, being injured was a minor inconvenience, however, with the benefit of hindsight, we now know that it was to cost him another record, that of the most consecutive League games played.

After returning to the side for the 1–0 home win against Queens Park Rangers on 3 April 1961, John would not miss another League game until the home game against Reading on 27 August 1968 – a run of 368 consecutive games. The all-time record was, and still is, held by Tranmere's Harold Bell, whose tally was 401 consecutive games. Had the injury not intervened and John had played throughout that first season, his final tally would have been a record breaking 406.

'It was frustrating because it would have been nice to have played in all the games in my first season, but I pulled the muscle in a game, and I couldn't have played in the next game, no matter how much I wanted to. I think the story given out may have been flu, but it wasn't – not sure now why we said it was.'

Swindon's start to the following campaign, 1961–62, put paid to any hopes they might have had of challenging for promotion. None of the first 10 games were won, and before the end of September they had conceded six goals on two occasions: away at Queens Park Rangers in a 6–1 defeat followed by a 6–2 thrashing at Barnsley three weeks later. In all, 29 goals were conceded in the first 10 games of the season.

'It was a terrible start. I can remember conceding lots of goals, and I particularly remember coming up against Queens Park Rangers. They had a winger called Mark Lazarus from a famous boxing family, and he absolutely ran me ragged. I was growing up quickly, remember I was just 18 and was still finding my feet.'

That poor run did, however, contain one collector's item: a goal for the young left-back. In his 770 League games John would not be a regular scorer, although a tally of 21 League goals wasn't a bad return for a left-back. That first goal came in a 3–1 defeat at Crystal Palace on 26 August 1961. I mention this to John, expecting this moment to be firmly etched on his brain, thus enabling him to give me a blow-by-blow account of the move that led to this momentous event. I am to be disappointed.

'I scored at Palace? Did I? I wish I could remember it. It would have been a big game as well, look at the gate! (25,000 – the highest gate John had played in front of at that stage in his career). No, I can't remember that at all I'm afraid. I do remember a fair few of my goals as I didn't get many, but obviously that one has slipped my mind.

One game I do remember was playing at Bradford Park Avenue, now of course long out of the League. There was a big, long tunnel running down from the dressing room to the pitch, and I can recall looking at Jimmy Scoular, who had been one of my heroes as a kid, and realising just how big he was. He had massive thighs I seem to remember. Anyway, Scoular was player-manager and he ran the show for them. His range of passing was superb, he just pinged the ball all the way around the pitch for them.'

Although the League form improved during October, there was a further shock in store for the team in the FA Cup. Not for the last time during John's time at the club, Swindon were knocked out by a non-League club, Kettering Town, who won 3–0 in a first-round replay.

'We should have won at Swindon really, but then any game away against a non-League club is always going to be difficult, even today. If you are a few yards off your normal game because the other side have raised their game then you are going to struggle, and that's what happened at Kettering.'

After that desperate start, the side did well to rally and finish ninth. Just four of the last 25 games were lost, and with the two Hunts, Ernie and Ralph, scoring 31 League goals between them, and there were signs that things were improving. Certainly, if you wanted goals Swindon were the team to watch – they scored 78 League goals but conceded 71. It was entertaining football.

'Back then the game really was very different to what it is today. It was much more spread out because most sides played with two wingers and there was only one centre-half. If you had attacking half-backs, like we did, often there would only be three of us back defending: Maurice Owen at centre-half and Terry and I as the full-backs. We had to do some serious covering behind Maurice at times. Even then, I still used to like to get forward. Then up front we had some very attacking-minded players like Ernie Hunt, Mike Summerbee, Arnold Darcy, Ralph Hunt, Cliff Jackson and Jack Smith. It's no wonder that we scored and conceded so many goals.

People tell me today that the game is much quicker. I think the reason for that is that players have much less of the pitch to cover, they all bunch up in the middle of the pitch and there's no width either. I've seen games recently where all 20 outfield players are standing in a small area either side of the halfway line and the centre circle waiting for the goalkeeper to kick it out – absolute madness!

I think I played in the best era for football, the 1960s. The game was entertaining because both sides went out to attack and play football, there was none of this "keep it tight" philosophy. The old

WM formation helped of course, but there was a different level of spirit in the game, both on and off the pitch, even down to fans from both sides standing together, which you wouldn't get today.'

The side was now taking shape, and the gamble Bert Head had taken in blooding the young players was to spectacularly pay off in the following season, 1962–63. For the first time since being admitted to the Football League in 1921, Swindon Town would gain promotion.

'You could see during the previous season that we were getting things right. If we hadn't had such a bad start we would have been much higher up the table then. We were definitely getting better as we got more experienced, the first season [1960–61] was really us finding our feet as youngsters but then in that second season we were starting to really gel together as a team. People like Bobby, Mike, Ernie, Cliff and Keith had all now been playing League football for three seasons, and Terry and I had now had a couple of years. We'd been kept together as a unit so we were used to playing with each other, and although one or two had moved on like Sam Burton and Bronco Layne the nucleus of the side was the same.'

Unlike the previous season, the team got off to a good start – just two of the first 13 matches were lost. The run included another early season goal for John, the first goal in a 2–0 home win over Hull City on 8 September. The side was increasingly settled, seven players missed only 10 games or fewer, unthinkable today in the squad rotation era, and, as is so often the case, a settled side proved to be a successful one.

For John, probably the most notable event of the season was the arrival of a new partner on the left side of the pitch – the man who would play in front of him for 10 seasons, Don Rogers. Rogers replaced Arthur Darcy for the home game with Southend United on 17 November, and although he only played seven times that season a firm friendship was formed, both on and off the pitch.

'I've got to say that in my first two seasons I've got a lot to thank two players for, who helped me settle into League football. One was Maurice Owen, who was a super fellow and really helped me and Terry Wollen, and the other was Arnold Darcy, who played in front of me on the left wing. Arthur was in some ways a bit more like one of today's "up and down" left-sided, midfield players, rather than a winger, because he was very good at tracking back and giving me support.

Then, of course, Don started to come on the scene, and, of course, he was a very different player because he played in the opponents half and didn't track back. Not that I'm complaining too much mind, because we played to his strengths by leaving him up front, and it also helped my game because I had to get used to defending different situations.'

As well as the good form in the League, there was also a good Cup run, in direct contrast to the previous year's shambles. Wins over Reading, Yeovil and Luton took 'The Town' to the fourth round where they met Everton at the County Ground. The First Division side were one of the best in the country (indeed they would win the Championship that season) and proved far too strong, rattling up a 4–0 half-time lead before winning 5–1.

'They were a great side, much too good for us. I was marking Billy Bingham who went on to manage Northern Ireland, and he scored twice. They were by far and away the best side I'd ever played against, and they gave us the runaround, but I suppose that was only to be expected.'

Back in the League things continued to go well despite a backlog of games caused by inclement weather. The side played eight games in April and didn't finish their League season until 18 May – commonplace today but very late back in those days. In the end, Roger Smart, like John, a locally-born youngster, scored the late winner against Shrewsbury at the County Ground on 14 May, which took Swindon into Division Two.

'The big thing about that year that everybody remembers was the terrible winter and all the snow that was around. There's no doubt about it, it really helped us get promotion – we were playing when people weren't, like that famous game against Queens Park Rangers when we played in basketball boots. To be fair to Bert, a lot of that was down to him – he wanted to get the games on so he would do things like clearing the pitch and getting us special boots, which meant we played more games during the big freeze, which lasted from Boxing Day through until March. I think it was Coventry who could have caught us, but they just ended up with too many matches to play.

It was the first time we'd ever got promoted as a club, of course, which made it very special, and I think it made a huge difference that so many of the team were locally born or had come through the club; somehow it made us more of a community, especially as most of the people who watched us were also born and raised in the town. The gates reflected that as well I think. I know that more people tended to watch football then, but for a town like Swindon to get over 20,000 people watching home games, as we did later on, when the town's population was under 100,000 was great. Nowadays, the town is much bigger, but fewer people have real allegiance to Swindon as a town – it's a changed town – you see lots of people in the town wearing Premiership teams' shirts not Swindon shirts, and the gates suffer as a result. Where are the supporters of the future for Swindon if all they are doing is supporting their Premiership sides by watching them on television all the time?'

So, after three seasons as a professional footballer, John, still not yet 20-years-old, had achieved what generations of Swindon footballers before him had tried and failed to do: he had played in a promotion-winning side. It was an auspicious start to a career.

FIRST-TEAM REGULAR... AND A RELEGATION

John was now a regular first-team player. Despite being just 20, he had played 136 League games and close on 150 first-team games in all competitions. He was ready for what was to be a major step up for the club. The fixture list for 1963–64 saw them pitted against the likes of Manchester City, Leeds and Newcastle, rather than Halifax, Wrexham and Bradford Park Avenue.

'It was unchartered territory really, obviously for the club because it had never played at that level before, but also, more importantly, for the players. Nowadays, when a side gets promotion a number of the players will have played at that level before in their careers, but if you look at our side we hadn't – all our League football had been played in the old Third Division. We were all looking forward to the challenge, of course, but we didn't really know what to expect.'

Nobody could have predicted Swindon's start to the season. The Division Two newcomers stormed into the new campaign, winning their first six games to sit proudly at the top of the table. Included in that run was a 3–0 win over Manchester City, yes Manchester City, a game that John still remembers as one of the best team performances that he ever played in.

'We went off on a great run at the beginning of the season – nine games unbeaten, and in that run was the game against Manchester

City that older supporters will still talk about as one of the best performances from any Swindon side – it was absolutely superb. I can't always remember the games I played in, but that Manchester City game will always stick in my mind – it just showed how good we were.'

Even though the run was ended with a 4–0 defeat at Northampton, only two of the first 15 games were lost as the youngsters took the Division by storm.

'I think we got a lot of confidence from the Manchester City game. We played without fear and got the results because of that. I do remember the Northampton game though – we got absolutely hammered, mainly because they were an old-fashioned lower division side who just kicked us and didn't let us play. There were some really hard players in that side – Kiernan, Branson, Theo Foley and a full-back called Mike Everitt who gave Mike Summerbee a very hard time. They really knocked us out of our stride. It was disappointing really because we had done so well against some of the big sides early on, Manchester City, Leeds, Sunderland and the like, so to lose to one of the Divisions lesser lights was frustrating.'

It was heady stuff. Swindon were the talk of the country and scouts flocked to see the young talent of Rogers, Hunt, Summerbee, Woodruff and Trollope.

'There were always lots of scouts. We were well known in the game as a good team to watch, and the fact that we started so well just meant that interest increased. Much of the focus was on Ernie Hunt and Mike Summerbee, although Don was also somebody who everybody talked about. Bobby Woodruff was one of the first to move, of course, and he was interesting scouts then as well. The papers were always talking up possible transfers, just like they do today. Not sure about me – there may have been interest, but if there was I was never told of it.'

It couldn't last. From the start of November through until the beginning of March only one game was won in the League, a 2–0 win over Portsmouth on 21 December. The team rallied a little, but, in all, only four

of the last 27 games were won as the season tailed off, and the team finished 14th.

'I think if you look at what happened we tended to struggle against some of the harder, more physical sides – most of us were 23 or under, so we perhaps didn't have the strength against those sides and got out-muscled. Also young players sometimes struggle for consistency, and there were so many of us in the team at the same time, so perhaps it was inevitable that our form would dip.'

As John flicks through the details of that season in the invaluable reference book of Paul Plowman, *Wembley and Beyond,* more memories come flooding back.

'We did find it tough didn't we? As the season went on – look at that, we lost 6–0 at Sunderland and 4–1 at Newcastle in February – 18 goals conceded that month in five games. I do recall Sunderland away. We got hammered, and I know Charlie Hurley, the centre-half, got at least two goals. It was the biggest crowd I'd played in front of – over 40,000.

At a personal level, though, I have to say I found it easier – there was more space to play. I think the good footballing players always find it easier to play at a higher level. If you watch lower division football now, and compare it to the Premiership, look at how much extra-time a Premiership footballer, particularly at one of the top teams, has on the ball. Often the player won't have anybody around them for 15 yards in the centre of midfield – even I could pass the ball well if you give me that amount of space! Looking back, the two years in the 1960s, and then the five years later which I spent in the Second Division, were the most enjoyable of my career from a footballing point of view because sides you played against were prepared to play football.'

The FA Cup again provided some respite. Wins over Manchester City and Aldershot set up a fifth-round tie with the eventual Cup winners, West Ham, at the County Ground. It was to be the first of three occasions that the teams were drawn together during John's playing career. The Hammers won 3–1.

'I don't remember this one as much as I remember the other two Cup ties, possibly because it was a long time ago and we lost. What I do recall is how the town reacted to any Cup run, even before the League Cup run. Swindon always had a bit of a reputation as a Cup town, and the fans used to enter into the spirit of the Cup, dressing up as Moonrakers and the like. Teams didn't like playing us because right the way through the 1960s we had some good players and could raise our game against big clubs by playing good football, not just by matching them for effort.'

The following season, 1964–65, began disastrously. An injury to goalkeeper Norman Oakley at Bury on the opening day of the season was a major factor in a 6–1 defeat as there were no goalkeepers on the substitutes bench in those days, indeed it was to be another season before substitutes of any kind would be introduced. Although the next two home games were won, five out of the next six games were lost. By the middle of September Swindon had conceded 22 goals.

'It was the reverse of the previous season because we got off to a terrible start. It wasn't all our own fault – Norman's injury didn't help, of course, and we never really recovered. Part of the issue was that we were still very attacking – that was Bert's way, of course – so it was a combination of the fact that you were still playing the old WM formation, which in its own way is attacking, coupled with the players who were playing which led to us perhaps being too attack-minded. I mean, if you look at the side, we replaced Bobby Woodruff with Roger Smart at left-half, and Roger was very attacking in that position. Often it was only Ken McPherson, Owen Dawson, Keith Morgan and I back. Perhaps the balance wasn't right.'

A run of four wins in the next seven games raised hopes of a revival, but the next five games were all lost, including an horrific 6–1 defeat at home to Newcastle United. In the middle of that run, John actually scored in successive home games, both in that Newcastle defeat and also in the 3–1 defeat by Bolton two weeks previously. Both goals were from the penalty spot, John taking over duties from Ernie Hunt who was missing through injury.

'We always practised taking penalties at training, and I slotted in a few at training so they said to me "you take them". I didn't volunteer. I don't think anyone else fancied it so it was given to me. I used to tend to put the penalties to the goalkeeper's left – remember I'm naturally right-footed, but then the later ones I put across my body into the left hand corner.'

One sad event was the retirement of Terry Wollen, the full-back who had made his debut with John back in 1960. Wollen had broken his leg against Notts County in the promotion-winning season of 1962–63, and although he had played a handful of games in 1963–64, and played a further couple of games in the early part of 1964–65, his League career was over at just 21. For John it was a personal blow.

'It affected me quite a lot really because Terry and I had played together for a long time, we'd come through Swindon Boys, the 'A' team, the youth team, the reserves and then the first team together. Terry was my roommate on away trips and we'd always been good mates. He was a different player to me, more cultured, and I have no doubt that he would have been good enough to have played at a higher level. I stayed in touch with him, and then he later came coaching with me.'

The season saw spells when the side looked as if they might pull clear, for example a run of four wins in five games around Christmas, but it was always going to be touch and go as to whether the second year in Division Two would be their last for the time being.

'We still had most of the youngsters, of course, only Bobby Woodruff had moved on, but the general view was that the spine of the side, goalkeeper, centre-half and centre-forward, needed strengthening. I'm not sure that I could see that at the time, but looking back now I can see that perhaps that spine wasn't strong enough. We needed, as youngsters, a bit more help and leadership from the spine of the team than we got. I don't know why changes weren't made, perhaps Bert was too loyal.'

In the end it all came down to the last day of the season and a scenario that still makes older Swindon supporters livid with rage. Swindon were a point ahead of fellow strugglers Portsmouth on the last day of the season. They, therefore, needed to better or equal the result of Portsmouth, who were playing at already promoted Northampton. Swindon themselves were also away, against Portsmouth's south-coast rivals Southampton, a top-five side but now out of the promotion picture. On paper the odds favoured Swindon. There was, however, one problem: Swindon's match would kick-off in the afternoon, Portsmouth's in the evening, thus Portsmouth would know exactly what they needed to do before kicking off and could plan accordingly.

'It was outrageous really. It should never have been allowed, and I think they changed the rules as a result of that. Not that it helped us. We felt cheated because they knew what they had to do. It's very different if you are 0–0 with 20 to minutes to go knowing you only need a point to being 0–0 with 20 minutes to go thinking you need to score.'

In the event, Swindon went down 2–1 to a late goal at the Dell. Portsmouth, now knowing they needed only a draw to survive, duly got the point they needed in a game that finished goalless. Swindon were relegated.

'We played quite well at Southampton, as I recall, and were unlucky to lose. However, once we lost we knew we were in trouble because, with Northampton already promoted, it was always likely that Portsmouth might get a point, which they did. Ironically, it was Jimmy Dickinson's last game for Portsmouth, and of course I later broke his record.

I still look back and think we should never have got relegated, it was just a season when we couldn't get going, just a bit more consistency and we would have been safe.'

As is so often the case, relegation led to some big changes at the club. By mid-September three of the more famous names at the club had moved on, Ernie Hunt to Wolves, Mike Summerbee to Manchester City and, most surprisingly of all, the manager and inspiration for much that Swindon had achieved during John's fledgling career, Bert Head. Head was sacked on 20 May 1965 after nine full seasons in charge.

'Nobody was surprised at Mike and Ernie moving on, especially as we had been relegated. They wanted to better themselves, and, whilst it was disappointing for those of us left behind, I don't think anybody blamed them. The real surprise was Bert Head being sacked. I was very shocked by that because he'd taken us up for the first time in the club's history and created a really good, young team. I know we'd been relegated, but I though that given his record he should have been given the chance to take us back up. I think he was very harshly treated.'

It was all change for John in the summer of 1965, not just a new manager but a new wife as well.

'I got married to Maureen in the summer of 1965, so it was my 40th wedding anniversary this year! We'd been together for something like four years before that so we knew each other well!'

The new manager was Danny Williams, a jovial Yorkshireman who had played 459 games for and then later managed Rotherham United. He was very much an unknown.

'Whenever a new manager is appointed, it's a time of uncertainty for all players. Will the new man like me? Can I prove myself to him? For many of us it was ever more unsettling because Bert Head was the only manager we'd ever known. He'd given us our chance, and we all felt that we owed him a lot because he was prepared to blood us so young and then stick by us.

I'd never heard of Danny Williams at all, and there was no speculation about who might get the job like there would be today. The first we knew about it was the day he was appointed. It took some getting used to because he was much less disciplined than Bert was in terms of how he liked to play football. It was much more off-the-cuff football.'

The new manager had some rebuilding to do. Over the next three seasons he would gradually assemble the side that was to have such great success at the end of the 1960s and beginning of the 1970s. First in was a goalkeeper who is still a close friend of John's today, nearly 40 years after they first played together, Peter Downsborough.

'Obviously I have a very soft spot for Pete because he was a good friend then and still is today – we still keep in regular contact. He wasn't a flamboyant goalkeeper, in fact he's not a flamboyant person, but he was a very good shot-stopper and an excellent goalkeeper. He saved us on many occasions

The other big signing at the time, although he didn't stay to play in the League Cup side, was Mel Nurse, who was very different to Peter. He was well known to all of us because he'd played for Wales, and was much more outgoing and charismatic. He was a good player to play with, a good footballer and a good bloke to have in the dressing room. I think it had been obvious that we needed to strengthen the spine of the side, and Peter and Mel went a long way to doing this.'

It was very much a period of transition for the team as new players came into the club, and others, including John's old Swindon Schoolboys mate Wilf Shergold, got their first taste of regular professional football. But, looking back, each season saw some critical additions: Downsborough, right-back Rod Thomas and midfielder/full-back Joe Butler played their first games in 1965–66, centre-half Stan Harland and midfielder Willie Penman the following season, and then winger Don Heath and striker Peter Noble in 1967–68.

'You could see what Danny was doing. Each season he'd bring in another couple of pieces of the jigsaw, based on where he thought we were short. If you look back on it, it was a textbook rebuilding job – do things gradually, blood the new players and then bring in another couple. He made some great signings as well, particularly by raiding the North-East for players like Wille Penman, Joe Butler and Peter Noble, who all came from Newcastle but weren't very well known.'

The three seasons of 1965–66, 1966–67 and 1967–68 in some ways can be grouped together. The side finished in similar sorts of positions: seventh, eighth and 10th respectively. They scored lots of goals: 74, 81 and 74 goals were the final tallies, but also conceded more than what would be expected of a promotion-winning side: 48, 59 and 51. They were great at home, losing 10 games in three seasons, but poor away, 17 victories in those three years was a relatively poor record. Don Rogers did his best with 67 League goals over the period, but it was a case of so near and yet so far.

'We were great to watch, particularly at home, and you always knew we'd score goals. Danny liked us to play attacking football, and it was under him that I really started to overlap on a regular basis. It's obvious where our problems were though, we were just too attacking, and we conceded far too many goals to challenge for promotion.'

For John personally, life continued very much as before. He was an automatic choice in the team and this was now towards the end of his run of 368 successive League games, although he did play three games out of position in 1965–66 as a midfielder, allowing first Joe Butler and then Rod Thomas, who, although a right-back, made his debut as a left-back, to fill the number-3 shirt.

'Rod was playing left-back in the reserves, and Danny said to me that he wanted to give Rod his debut before the end of the season, and that, because it was his debut, he didn't want to play him out of position, and so would I play in midfield. I agreed, of course, but I wasn't very keen. By now I was used to playing left-back and thought it was my position. Anyway, I needn't have worried because the following season Rod forced himself into the team as right-back, and I got my position back.'

Season 1965–66 was a memorable one for John in that it was his best-ever season in terms of League goals scored. He could usually be relied upon to chip in with a goal or two over the course of a season (other than his first season as a professional, there were only three other seasons, 1963–64, 1970–71 and 1973–74, when he didn't score a single League goal) but no more than that. In 1965–66, though, he scored the magnificent total of three, helped by the fact that with Ernie Hunt having moved on he was now the regular penalty taker.

'I never minded taking penalties, but in the end I missed a couple and they said "why have we got a full-back taking the penalties – let's give them to Don!" I do recall missing one at the Town End, against Swansea I think, when I side footed the ball past the post – that was embarrassing. The one goal I do remember was at Mansfield [April 1966]. Owen Dawson and I both scored within a couple of minutes of each other. It was the quickest goals ever scored by full-backs in a League game. We won 5–1, that was one of our good days!'

I also, and I think few people know this, had one first-team game as a striker. We played at Oldham in the 1965–66 season, and we were very short of forwards so Danny said to me "you're fit- just go and run around up front and cause them some problems." I really enjoyed it, but I didn't score and then the strikers were fit again, so that was the end of that.'

Despite the frustrations in the League, there was still the Cup competitions, and Swindon were by now recognised as one of those tricky, lower division sides that teams didn't want to be drawn against. This was best illustrated in the FA Cup run of 1966–67, a run that put the team back on the footballing map and gave a foretaste of the potential that was to be cemented in two years time.

'That was a brilliant Cup run, everyone still talks about playing at Upton Park in the mud when West Ham were one of the best teams in the country. It was just after the World Cup win so everyone was talking about Moore, Hurst and Peters. We should have won but Geoff Hurst rescued them. Then, at Swindon, we played very well again and deserved to win. It was quite an achievement to be the better side against a First Division side in two games – it showed the potential of the side.

Then it was Nottingham Forest, again they were a very good side. I think they were runners-up that season [they were]. Again, what was encouraging was the fact that we held our own in two games against them. Sometimes you catch a bigger team on a bad day and get a result, but to hold them twice [0–0 at Nottingham and 1–1 at Swindon] was tremendous. We got well beaten at Villa Park in the end [in the second replay] but even then the scoreline flattered them a bit.

Around this time we were at our best against the better teams, which showed the potential of the players and the club. I think much of this was down to the fact that better teams let you play a bit more, and when we were allowed to play we were very good. Perhaps we were a bit inconsistent in the League when we came up against some of the sides who didn't let us play, particularly away.'

Despite the inconsistency of the three seasons immediately after relegation, there was a sense in the town that Danny Williams was building a good side. Each year Swindon were one of the fancied sides, usually with the caveat 'if they can keep hold of Don Rogers'. The players certainly felt they were getting better, as John explains:

'We all felt we had a better quality of player than most of the teams in the League. If you look at the side by the end of 1967–68 we had players like Don, Rod, Stan Harland and Peter Noble, all of whom would go on and play in the top flight. It was frustrating that we were inconsistent, but we knew that if we could tighten up the defence promotion was there for the taking.'

The following season, with the defence duly tightened, was to be the greatest year in the history of the club to date.

AN UNLUCKY BREAK

As had been the case over the previous four years, Danny Williams entered the transfer market during the summer of 1968. This year the three signings were Chris Jones, a striker from Manchester City, John Smith, a midfielder from Torquay United, and Frank Burrows, a centre-half from Scunthorpe United. Jones would play only occasionally during the season, but, as John explains, the other two were key signings.

'Both John and Frank were very important signings – the final pieces in the jigsaw really. Frank Burrows was a very different type of centre-half from Mel Nurse, and to be honest was probably what we needed. Mel was a good, ball-playing centre-half. He'd played at a higher level, and he was good at bringing the ball from the back. Frank, as I'm sure he won't mind me saying, was a good, old-fashioned centre-half in many ways, in a sense a lower division centre-half in that that's where he'd played his career, but he was much more aggressive and he really toughened us up. In a real sense Frank was our leader, because although Stan Harland was the captain, and a good captain too, it was Frank who was the one who let you know when you weren't doing it on the pitch, he was a real growler! All credit to Danny Williams, though, because although I'd never heard of Frank before he signed he was a critical signing for us.

John Smith was very important too. He was a good playmaker, an old fashioned "midfield general" if you like. He could spray the ball round, and although he would be the first to admit that he didn't do much running he had Joe Butler and Roger Smart, two very fit lads, to do his running for him. He could look after himself as well – he was an experienced professional, and I think what Danny had seen, with us being good to watch but perhaps too easy to beat, was that we needed the steel that Frank and John would give us.'

So a new season kicked off with 'the Town' at home to Stockport County. John, as always, was at left-back, indeed, with the exception of the fact that Chris Jones played instead of Joe Butler, the starting line up was the same as that which would grace Wembley later in the season. Swindon won that game 1–0, and John duly completed his 367th consecutive League appearance. By now he was just 35 games away from beating the record for the most consecutive League games played, he was on target to achieve this before the end of the season, but was he aware of the record?

'I think it would have been impossible not to be aware of the record. Each season the local press would make some comment, and, of course, there were the little milestones along the way that got some mention, like 250 consecutive games, 300, 350 and so on. The pen pictures of us in the matchday programme when we went to away grounds always used to mention the run as well. I was lucky though because, not only did I not have any injuries for a period, the managers I played for used to like me, so I was always selected as well.'

It wasn't to be. The following week Swindon were away at Hartlepool. The match ended in a 0–0 draw, but it was overshadowed by an injury to John which would mean his chance of setting a new record would end. Coincidentally, that game at Hartlepool was the first game missed by John's regular left-flank companion Don Rogers in 181 League games, another remarkable achievement.

'I can remember the injury as if it was yesterday. A ball came towards me from their defence in the air, I jumped with their big centre-half, whose name I've forgotten, and as we fell he landed on top of me and my arm went over at an angle. It went numb, but I carried on playing, and it wasn't until I took a throw-in, or should I say tried to take a throw-in, a couple of minutes later that I realised there was a real problem. I really knew I'd done something when Harry Cousins told me I'd have to come off. Harry was a tough man, and if he told you to come off there was definitely a problem.

Anyway, I went to the hospital at Hartlepool, but they wouldn't touch it – they said it was a bad break and it needed more medical attention than they were prepared to give. So I travelled all the way back on the coach to Swindon with my arm in a sling – not very comfortable I can tell you! On the Sunday I went up to the old Princess Margaret Hospital in Swindon, and they called a surgeon out to have a look. Harry Cousins said I must have been famous for them to have got a surgeon out on a Sunday – in those days people didn't work on Sundays!

They operated in midweek and put a plate in the arm. They said they'd take the plate out when it got uncomfortable. Thirty seven years on the plate is still there, it's never given me any trouble.'

The initial prognosis was that John would be out of action for 12 weeks. It was a frustrating time, particularly as the club started to realise their potential, with excellent form in both the League and the League Cup. Much of this was down to the revamped defence. Frank Burrows made an immediate impact at centre-half, and Rod Thomas did a good job deputising for the injured John, with Owen Dawson coming in at right-back to replace Thomas. The result was that the team kept eight clean sheets in their first 10 matches, and by Christmas had only conceded 15 goals in 20 League games. Of those goals, only two were conceded at home, a remarkable record. Ironic, isn't it, one of Swindon's best defensive spells in John's time at the club came when he was out of action. John, a very self-effacing man, can see the funny side

'It's great isn't it, as soon as I'm out of the side we stop conceding goals! There is a more serious explanation to that, though, from a footballing perspective, and it's this: Owen, who came in to replace me, was a much more defensive player than me, he didn't used to overlap like I did. Rod was also quite defensively minded as well, and with Frank coming in to organise us, and with the consistency of Peter Downsborough and Stan Harland in the defence as well, it's no surprise we did so well. Frank always used to say we were a better unit without me in the team!'

Despite the excellent League form, the talk of the town was not of promotion but of Wembley. Against all the odds, Swindon had reached the League Cup Final, beating Torquay United (a game in which John played as it took place between the first two League games of the season), Bradford City, Blackburn Rovers, Coventry City, Derby County and Burnley. John had seen it all from the touchline.

'It was the biggest disappointment of my career, the most successful season in my time at the club, and I missed half of it. Of course I watched all the games. Danny was brilliant at keeping me involved, but it wasn't the same as playing. You're involved, but you're not involved because you're not out there on the pitch.

In terms of the Cup run, various things stand out. Firstly, it was nearly all over before it started. We were very lucky to beat Bradford City in the second round, they should have won really, and in some ways that was the hardest game that we had in the entire Cup run. Then, looking back, we played so many matches, replay after replay. It was tough for the lads who played, particularly given the fact that we really only used 14 players or so all season. You also look back at the quality of sides that we played. We beat a First Division side in Coventry, a very good Second Division side in Derby and then a top First Division side in Burnley – it wasn't exactly an easy run to the Final! You do realise, now, with the benefit of hindsight, that we had some really good players; most could have played in the First Division, not just those who eventually got the opportunity to do so like Rod, Stan, Peter Noble and Don.

The game I will never forget was the game against Burnley at The Hawthorns in the replay. We'd won up there, then they'd won down at our place – a game I remember most for the physical battle in midfield between Colin Blunt and John Smith, so it was off to a third game. That night we really showed our character, one of the big strengths of the team, we never knew when we were beaten. To concede a goal so close to the end of the game to lose the lead and then to go behind so early in extra-time but still to come back and win was fantastic.'

One might have thought that John, with eight seasons of being the first choice left-back, would be immediately put back in the team when he was fit again. However, that wasn't the case. As we have seen, the team were doing well in John's absence; in particular the defence, which was tighter in terms of goals conceded than in any season since John had been associated with the club. Owen Dawson was doing well. He couldn't get back in.

'I couldn't really complain, despite having been first choice for so long before the injury. The team were doing really well and the defence in particular was playing well. Danny couldn't be faulted for not wanting to change a winning side, and, to be fair, Owen had settled in very well.

It was frustrating though. I actually thought I was fit enough to play before I did. I kept fit by running in my sling and doing some training when Harry Cousins wasn't watching. However, Harry and the club doctor weren't keen on me playing before Christmas. They wanted to make sure everything healed well before letting me go back.'

John made his return to first-team action as a substitute (in midfield!) in the home game against Tranmere on 18 January 1969, in a game that finished goalless. Still, there was no way of getting back into the team, until fate played a hand. Owen Dawson, who seemed to have made the place his own, was himself injured during a 5–1 win at home to Oldham Athletic on 28 January 1969. The next week, for the 1–1 draw at Barnsley, John was back. He even marked his return with an early goal!

'There is no doubt that had Owen been fit for the Cup Final he would have played. I was very lucky in that he got his injury. He injured his back and couldn't play. Even with that injury, had he recovered in time he would have come back into the team ahead of me, I'm absolutely sure of that, because Danny was a very loyal manager and would have tried to have played the players who had got us to Wembley in the Cup Final.

I do remember the goal at Barnsley, it's one of the few I can recall. I cut in from the left and fired it across the goalkeeper into the net. A goal after eight minutes, I bet Frank Burrows went mad with the fact that I was up in the opponent's penalty area when I should have been defending! It does show my view on football though, both as a player and a manager I never liked shutting up shop, I'd rather we tried things and lost rather than play for a boring draw. For me, football is entertainment, and we shouldn't forget our obligation to the paying public, plus, of course, it's much more rewarding to play the game that way.'

Unlucky Dawson, lucky John. Such is football, and although it would have been very harsh if John, after playing so many games without a gap (I was going to write break but decided it would be in poor taste), had missed the big day at Wembley there is no doubt that he would have done had Dawson not got injured.

Back in the side, John fitted back into what was now a very solid unit. In his first seven games back the team conceded just two League goals and kept five successive clean sheets. They were unbeaten in those seven League games as well. Indeed, the first time they lost in 1969 was in a midweek game at Gillingham on 5 March. They lost on the following Saturday as well, 2–1 at Stockport, in a game played a week before the League Cup Final. Was it Cup Final nerves?

'I think inevitably we lost half a yard or so of pace because we were thinking about Wembley and nobody wanted to miss out on the big day because of injury. We all knew that this could well be our one big chance – nobody would ever expect us to get there again – so although people weren't pulling out of challenges or anything like that, it was always on your mind. I'm sure that contributed to our defeats.'

And so to Saturday 15 March 1969, the biggest match in the club's history to date. Swindon had, remarkably, reached the semi-finals of the FA Cup before, twice in fact, when they had been a Southern League club in the early 1900s. This, though, was a showpiece Final.

Their opponents, Arsenal, were firm favourites. Not only did they have a two division status advantage over the Wiltshire upstarts, but most of their team were used to Wembley, having played in the 1–0 defeat by Leeds United in the previous seasons League Cup Final. By contrast, for all of the Swindon players it was their first appearance at 'the Twin Towers'.

'The week before the Final was just mad really. There was so much radio, press and television interest, which of course for most of us was all very new. The whole town seemed to want to wish us luck. We did lots of promotional things in shops around the town, it all seemed a little bit unreal really.

We travelled up on the Friday and went to Gerrards Cross to stay in a hotel. I know we all tried to follow our usual routines before a game, so those people who wanted breakfast had breakfast, those who usually slept in, slept in and so on. I know I slept fine, and I don't remember being particularly nervous. In the dressing room at Wembley, again, we followed our own routines, so I just sat quietly in the corner getting myself ready for the game. I tended not to want people round me before a game, and I certainly wasn't a shouter or a motivator like some!'

The story of the match will be familiar enough to all Swindon fans, indeed, to most football fans of a certain age anywhere. The underdogs won, becoming only the second Third Division side to win a major Cup Final, a record which still stands. The bare facts of the game, Roger Smart put Swindon ahead in the first half, Bobby Gould equalised for Arsenal four minutes from time and then two goals by Don Rogers in extra-time sealed Swindon's win, tell only half the story.

'I can remember being skinned for the first 20 minutes by John Radford. If you look at the video of the match they dominated the first part of the game and most of their attacks came down my side. It did take me a while to settle down, but once I did then I was happy with the way I played.

There is no doubt that the pitch helped us. It was very, very heavy and difficult to play on right from the start, let alone after extra-time. There had been a lot of talk about the flu bug in the Arsenal camp the week before the game, and Danny used that in his talk before extra-time. We were obviously disappointed by conceding such a late goal, but Danny simply emphasised that we'd matched them so far and would now be fitter than they were. Part of this was down to their flu bug, but it shouldn't be forgotten that we were a very fit side indeed.

As for extra-time, well it was all about Donald. Everyone talks about his second goal when he ran from the halfway line and then did that great dummy past Bob Wilson, but in fact I think his first goal is better than most people give him credit for. He managed to get the ball out from under his feet extremely well.

Everyone will always remember the game as Donald's day because of the goals, and rightly so, but don't forget how important Peter Downsborough was to us that day. He kept us in the game when we were under the cosh, and without him there might never have been any extra-time.'

For some of the Swindon team, while this was one of the big days of their career, other great days would follow. For example, Rod Thomas would win a First Division Championship medal with Derby County, Don Rogers would, all too briefly, be the talk of the country while at Crystal Palace and Peter Noble would score regularly in the top flight for Burnley. For John, though, destined to spend his entire career at Swindon, this was the biggest day of his footballing life.

'It was a great day, clearly my best day in football. I took more professional pride in the two promotions in a way because they were about consistency over a season, but this was the peak of my career from the point of view of a one-off game. Nobody expects to play in a side that wins at Wembley when you are a lower division footballer. It did go very quickly though. I know everybody says that's the case, but for me it was very true. I suppose you are so focused on playing the game that you can't necessarily take in everything.'

After the match there were celebrations and the homecoming. What does John remember about them?

'We had a great party in London the night after the game. I still don't think it had sunk in that we had won and what an achievement it was. In some ways, we were relieved that it had gone well, and we had done ourselves justice and were more thinking about that than the fact we had won.

I'll never forget coming back to Swindon on the Sunday. As we got closer to Swindon, the bridges on the M4 seemed to have more and more people on them to welcome us, and then as we made our way into Swindon the whole town seemed to have come out to see us. It was just a sea of people – incredible really.'

After Wembley, back to the League. Perhaps unsurprisingly, the week after the Cup Final the side lost again in the League, 2–1 at Plymouth, making it three League defeats in a row. The following week, after a midweek home win over Barnsley, there was another, more damaging defeat when Watford, Swindon's closest challengers for the Third Division title, won 1–0 at the County Ground, in front of nearly 30,000 people.

'We were just glad to get the first game out of the way really, and I think it was always likely that there would be some sort of 'Wembley Hangover' or whatever you wanted to call it. I remember that Plymouth were really 'up' for the game. They always saw us as a derby game anyway, and now we were a team that everybody wanted to beat.

The Watford game was very annoying. I know that throughout my time at Swindon there was always a sense from fans that we tended not to perform at home on the very big games, and I suppose this was an example. I don't remember a huge amount about the game itself, except that we should have got at least a draw. We were the best side in the Division that year, and it's frustrating that we didn't win the Championship. It was this game that cost us.'

The Watford setback was to be the last defeat of the season. The team were unbeaten for the last nine League games, clinching promotion when Chris Jones scored a late goal at Rotherham on 2 May to secure a 1–1 draw. However, that point was won without John, who played against Bristol Rovers on 12 April but then missed four games of the run-in, returning only for the final game of the season, a 2–0 win over Barrow on 5 May.

I assume that John missed those games through injury, a final blow in what had been a difficult season personally and perhaps some sort of balancing of the books for eight injury-free seasons. However, I am wrong.

'I don't think I was injured. I was injured so rarely in my career that I remember those occasions. No, I think I was dropped! Next time I see Danny I must ask him what that was all about, although I see that we kept a run of clean sheets without me! I was only dropped on one other occasion, that was under Les Allen when I refused to play long balls, but we'll come to that later.'

It had been a frustrating season for John. His total of just 19 League appearances was by some way the fewest of any full season in which he played. However, that frustration was tempered by the success of the side, they were promoted back to the Second Division, missing out on the Championship to Watford only on goal average, and were winners of the League Cup. The reason for the success could be tracked down to one key area: a much improved defensive record. Just seven goals were conceded at home in 23 League games and 35 in all, the fewest goals conceded in any season that John played at Swindon. When I share this statistic with John it prompts another good humoured reflection.

'Don't ever tell Frank Burrows that statistic, he'd say it was down to the fact that I wasn't in the side that we conceded so few goals. He was always complaining that I spent too much time attacking and not enough defending [this is factually true, as when I'd interviewed Frank as part of my research for a book on Don Rogers he made the point, in his thick Scottish accent, that John was 'always overlapping']. In my defence, I would say that although I got up the pitch quickly, I also ran back fast as well. Mind you, with Frank growling at you, you'd do the same

The defence was clearly a major part in our success. We said before that Frank was a key signing, and the fact that we weren't conceding as many goals meant that we were under less pressure to score. In fact, we won a lot of games that season 1–0, which was a very unlike Swindon result. When I say defence I don't just mean the back five because people like Joe Butler and Roger Smart were very important in terms of the defensive work that they did. Danny should take credit too because he did things that others might not have thought of, like playing Joe, who was left footed, on the right, and Roger, who was right footed, on the left. It was a hard system to play against. I suppose you'd call it 4–3–3 today, but we were very flexible, and because we were a very fit side we could break very quickly.

The other thing that helped us that season was that we had played together for a while and were used to each other's game. Danny had built the side up gradually, so although there were a couple of new faces each year to keep things fresh there was a nucleus of players who had been there for a while, which also helped team spirit. Danny's strength was in spotting players who would play as a team. As Real Madrid have shown, it's not always the best individual players who make the best team, and signing players who weren't high profile, but would do a great job for the club created a successful team. He made very, very few signings that didn't work out.'

It had been a great season. Now for another assault on Division Two!

BACK IN THE SECOND

During the summer of 1969 there was a genuine belief among both players and supporters that Swindon Town had a chance of going straight through the Second Division and into the First Division. Heady expectations for a club that had only previously spent two seasons outside the bottom two divisions of English football during their near 90 years' existence.

Yet those expectations were based not just on blind optimism, but on some solid facts. The team had a settled look – during the summer of 1969 there was just one acquisition, centre-forward Arthur Horsefield, signed from Middlesbrough as support for Peter Noble, and none of the promotion-winning side had left. There are many instances of successful, settled sides getting into the 'winning habit' and achieving successive promotions – John's view is that this was a real chance for Swindon to become another.

'We all thought we had a real chance of going up again. The team had stayed together, which was a big plus, and we had a lot of players who had good League experience and were now in their mid-20s when they were approaching their peak – people like myself, Joe Butler, Roger Smart, Don Rogers, Rod Thomas, Frank Burrows, Peter Noble and Peter Downsborough were all born within a couple of years of each other. We should have gone up, there's no doubt about it – the team was good enough to play at a higher level, as was proved by the fact that a number of that side did go on to play in the First Division with other clubs. Some of the players who didn't get that opportunity could have done as well.'

There was, however, one major change – in the manager's office. Danny Williams, after his success the previous season, had become a wanted man, and in the end the lure of going back to his native Yorkshire and managing

First Division Sheffield Wednesday proved too much. At the time, it was a major shock to most people at the club, although John says he wasn't one of those who fitted into that category

'I don't think I was that surprised really. Danny had attracted a lot of attention because of what the team had achieved over the previous season, and, just like today, clubs were always looking out for bright, young managers. I think the fact that the club that he moved to was in Yorkshire was no surprise either because Danny was still very popular in the area because of his connections with Rotherham; you've also got to remember that Sheffield Wednesday were a big club then – a First Division club. We didn't blame him for leaving, I think everyone has the right to try and better themselves if they can.'

Danny's replacement would be someone well known to the players, Fred Ford, who had previously been first-team coach at the club before leaving to join Bristol Rovers. This seemed a good move – the players all liked and respected Ford, and it seemed to give the club the continuity it needed. If it ain't broke…

'The club handled the situation well, I thought. There were only a couple of days between Danny leaving and Fred being appointed so it wasn't as if there was much time for anyone to be unsettled by what had happened. Fred was a good appointment as well; he was well respected by the players because of what he had done when he was with us before, and I still say he was the best coach I worked under.

For me personally it was good news; you always wonder whether a new manager will take to you as a player, and, although I was very lucky in that regard in my career, the fact that I knew Fred and he knew me meant I would be OK.'

Thirty-five years on, it seems odd to describe a season where Swindon finished fifth in the Second Division, reached the sixth round of the FA Cup and won the Anglo-Italian Cup as a disappointment. It was comfortably their best-ever League position, and, if one excludes the two runs to the FA Cup semi-finals as a non-League team when the FA Cup had far fewer teams competing, their best ever FA Cup run. Moreover, to win the Anglo-Italian Cup they beat Juventus, yes Juventus, twice, at home and away. So why was the season a disappointment?

'We should have gone up, and we knew it. That away record stopped us going up – just four wins – together with the fact that we drew too many games [seven at home and nine away]. The truth is that we underachieved that season – it was the year when the team were at their peak, and we adapted very well to a higher division. I'm still disappointed looking back; I would have loved to have played in the First Division, and that was my chance. I also think that the team would have done very well in the First Division – we'd shown we could play well against the top teams in the cup competitions, and, whilst they are a one-off, we would have been fine because the quality was there across the team.'

The team had begun the season well, with just three defeats in the first 13 games, but really put themselves into the promotion picture with an unbeaten run that lasted from 29 November through until 30 March – a run of 14 games. The crucial game was against Blackpool at home, in front of nearly 30,000 at the County Ground on 7 April. Arthur Horsefield gave the home side a first-minute lead, but the visitors, who would go on to secure promotion, equalised, and when Middlesbrough ended Swindon's unbeaten home record for the season the following week the promotion dream was over.

'If you look back, it wasn't just those two games that cost us, it was the final run in – I seem to remember that we had a bad overall finish [this is true, just two wins from the final six games]. Didn't we lose at Millwall? [They did, 3–1, on 4 April, four games from the end of the season.] That was a horrible place to play, the Den, absolutely terrible. The tunnel used to be behind the goal, and you'd come out and the verbal abuse would be incredible – there would be people screaming at you, spitting at you, just trying to intimidate you, I don't think any visiting player liked playing there. Then those two home games against Blackpool and Middlesbrough – the Blackpool one was the key game really. Had we won that I still think we would have gone up; by the time we played the following week against Middlesbrough I think we knew that the dream was over, and I'm sure that had an impact on the result.'

The League Cup defence ended disappointingly with a 1–0 reversal at local rivals Oxford United in round three, but some solace was found in the FA Cup run, which saw Blackburn, Chester and Scunthorpe beaten, before a sixth-round tie with Leeds United at the County Ground. This was the era of the great Leeds side under the management of Don Revie, and the visitors, with the likes of Jack Charlton, Norman Hunter, Billy Bremner, Johnny Giles and Allan Clarke playing, were too strong, winning 2–0.

'You always like putting yourself up against the bigger teams, just to see how you stand up with them. Leeds, though, were desperately difficult to play against – not only were they a good football side, but they were ultra professional, which made them harder to beat. We always fancied our chances against someone like West Ham, who would play football but might not battle as much as we would, but there was no way that we were going to outbattle Leeds.'

In the end, the big triumph of the season was to be in 'European' football. This, in its own way, was slightly odd. Swindon, as winners of the League Cup, should have had entry into the old Fairs Cup (now the UEFA Cup), but, for reasons that seem as incomprehensible now as they did at the time, they were denied entry (as Queens Park Rangers had been two years earlier) because they had been a Third Division side when they won the trophy. So John and his teammates found themselves instead playing two competitions against Italian clubs.

The first competition was the spurious and short-lived Anglo-Italian Cup Winners' Cup. Played between the winners of the Italian Cup, AS Roma, and Swindon, the match, played over two legs, took place at the start of the 1969–70 season. Swindon lost the first leg in Rome 2–1 but triumphed convincingly at the County Ground, winning 4–0, largely due to a hat-trick by Arthur Horsefield. A trophy it might be, but the Swindon public were not convinced – just under 15,000 turned out for the second leg, well below the season's League average. By contrast, 40,000 had seen the first leg in Italy.

'It was a great experience to play in the Olympic Stadium in Rome – a big crowd – I think the Italians took the competition more seriously than we did – and a great atmosphere. Back at Swindon we absolutely hammered them, playing a British game if you like. They didn't know how to cope with our energy and pace – I remember Don and Pete Noble really relished it that night. We were tight at the back as well, although back then the Italian teams tended to be more cautious than they are today.'

The second competition was the Anglo-Italian Cup. In its own way equally spurious, this was competed for by six English clubs and six Italian clubs. The rules were complex, but essentially the 12 clubs were split into three groups with two Italian and two English clubs in each group. The two English sides then played the two Italian sides in their group home and away, but didn't play each other, thus leaving a mini-league table, which showed four games played. The English team with the best record from the group stage then played the Italian team with the best record in the Final. Got that? Good. It's no wonder that with such a convoluted approach the competition didn't last long.

The Anglo-Italian Cup was played at the end of the season, and Swindon found themselves drawn with S.S Napoli and the mighty Juventus. Quite what the mighty Juve were doing playing in this competition is not clear. They were, as now, a major force in Italian, and indeed European, football. To prove that point, they would reach the Final of the Fairs Cup (now the UEFA Cup) the following season, losing only to Leeds United. The Swindon fans had their own chance to see how good Juventus were when they visited the County Ground on 2 May, however, perhaps because the football season had finished in many people's minds (this was at a time when the League season was always scheduled to end in April) or perhaps because the public weren't convinced of the value of the competition, just 12,879 bothered to turn up. Those who missed the game, therefore, weren't present for an astonishing result – Swindon Town 4 Juventus 0.

'It's fantastic isn't it? We played some of the very best Italian teams and beat them, just shows how good we were, and that we would have done very well had we got promotion. I really enjoyed the games – a chance to play on some great grounds and against a very different style of football.

I think it also showed that we would have done well had we been allowed to play in the Fairs Cup – the Italian sides were some of the best in Europe then, as they are today, so just imagine what we would have been like against some of the lesser lights. It was very wrong that we weren't allowed into the Fairs Cup. If you win a competition then you should be allowed to enter into the event that you've earned the right to participate in. It was outrageous really.'

A week later S.S Napoli came to the County Ground. Even fewer – just over 10,000 – attended, and this time Swindon were beaten, despite a John Smith goal, losing 2–1 to a team they would become very familiar with. And so to Italy. The matches were played on a once-a-week basis so the team knew they would be in Italy for a while when they flew out ahead of their game with Juventus in Turin on 16 May. This tournament, which ended up taking up the whole of May, was eating into one of their two months off over the summer. Did the players resent it?

'No, we didn't resent it, we had a great time. We were all keen to have the experience of playing against a different style of team, and, let's face it, Italy wasn't a bad place to be for two weeks or so. We had a good time – remember we all got on very well as a team – and had tournaments, especially a big tennis tournament, and just relaxed on the beach. Looking back, it was odd preparation in a way because I know that Napoli were doing the traditional Italian pre-match ritual of training up in the hills. It didn't seem to hurt us though, everyone was sensible, apart from Fred Ford who didn't follow his own advice to drink only bottled water and was violently ill, much to our amusement.'

Remarkably, both matches in Italy were won: a 1–0 win over Juventus followed by a win by the same score over S.S Napoli. These results meant that Swindon had the best record of any of the English sides competing in the competition. They would, therefore, play in the Final against S.S Napoli, who, by a quirk of fate, were the Italian team with the best record.

The Final took place in Naples on 27 May 1970. The Italians clearly saw

this as a bigger priority than their English counterparts as 55,000 attended the Final, but their passion was to have an unpleasant side, as, with Swindon leading 3–0 with 10 minutes to go, the crowd rioted and the game was abandoned, with the Cup being awarded to Swindon.

'We'd won the game by the time the riot started, and I guess that's one of the reasons why the problems happened – the Italian fans were fed up with their team. The riot was on my side of the pitch – it started with soft things being thrown and then the slabs started to come over the fence. It was pretty scary really. I think I realised we were in trouble when I looked up to pass to Donald and he was on the other side of the pitch! Gradually the play just moved over to one side – the side furthest away from the riot, and in the end it became so farcical that they had to take us off.

The problem, once it was evident that the game wasn't going to restart, was how to get off the pitch once we'd been presented with the Cup because the dressing rooms were on the same side as the riot. In the end, Fred led the way – he just lifted the Cup onto his head and made a dash for it!'

It is easy to ridicule the Anglo-Italian Cup – many have done it, including me. However, on the more positive side, this was a triumph which reflected very positively on the club and the players. It was proof that the team were a class act and First Division quality. They had come close to promotion; they had shown they could hold their own against European opposition and they were a settled, cohesive unit. The future looked bright.

It was the peak of that side. We were so settled. If you look at the record books I think most of us played in virtually every game [John is right. Ten players played 36 or more games, a remarkable record]. We were disappointed not to have gone up, but the team was still together and we were young enough to have another go. We really thought that the following year we would make it.'

For John personally things had gone well. Now free of injury, he had resumed his rightful place at left-back and had played in all 54 of Swindon's competitive fixtures. He had even found time to score a couple of goals: at Sheffield United in a 2–1 win and the only goal in a 1–0 win over Watford at the County Ground.

'As we've discovered, I don't always remember my goals, but I can remember those two goals very well. Against Watford I cut in from the left and drove it low and hard into the bottom corner, and then at Sheffield I scored with a header – I think it was my only ever headed goal. I enjoyed the season though, I thought it was one of my best because, like most of the rest of the team, I played better against the better players – you get more time to play and generally the other sides try to play football, which makes for a better game.

It was the closest that I ever came to playing in the First Division. I would have loved to have played there, but I think realistically it would have had to have been with Swindon at that stage because I'm not sure that anybody would have taken a chance on me given my age. I certainly never heard about anyone coming in for me, not that the club would necessarily have told me. Could I have played there? Possibly, I guess it's for others to say. I could do the basics well, and I had a lot of energy, and I was fortunate in that Fred, and Danny before me, encouraged me to focus on the things I could do well.'

It is one of the great mysteries in the history of Swindon Town football club as to why the side failed to push on from their successful 1969–70 season. With the benefit of hindsight, 1970 saw the team at the peak of their powers; over the next four seasons there would be a slow decline, leading to relegation back to Division Three in 1973–74. Initially, it wasn't as if it was due to the fact that players had left. The team that lined up for the opening day draw with Hull City at the County Ground was a familiar one: Downsborough, Thomas, Burrows, Harland, Trollope, Butler, Smith, Smart, Rogers, Horsefield and Noble. Ten of that side had played at Wembley (Don Heath being the only absentee), and it was the same side that had won the Anglo-Italian Cup in the summer. Yet the team never remotely threatened promotion that season. Why?

'I wish I could tell you why we didn't push on. Looking back, perhaps Fred was just too loyal to the players who had served us well. Although he brought in Arthur Horsefield in that first season and then Steve Peplow the following year, he didn't change it much. It would have been hard to have done that though, because things had gone so well. We were still very good at our best, but I think we had a few more injuries that season, and maybe the players who came in just weren't as good as the players they replaced – not just as players, but also perhaps they weren't as good mentally, in terms of having a winning mentality, which I felt the side had from 1968 to 1970.'

Part of the reason is clear from the League table. The team returned to their old habits of being great at home but lousy away. Only two of the 21 home League games were lost and, conversely, only three of the 21 away League games were won.

'It was a terrible away record, wasn't it? I hadn't realised it was quite that bad. I wish I knew the answer as to why, and I bet Fred did at the time as well because it was very frustrating. With a half-decent away record we would have been challenging for promotion again.'

There was at least one good night during the season, a reminder perhaps of the quality of the team. It came in the League Cup Third Round when, on 6 October, Liverpool visited the County Ground. This was a developing Liverpool side under Bill Shankly, not the force they would become later in the decade, but still a side good enough to reach the FA Cup Final that season. They would have expected to have won at what was now a mid-table Division Two side, but they didn't as two goals from Don Rogers gave Swindon a 2–0 win.

'There is the proof that we could still do it. Liverpool was a great scalp for us. The only thing I can remember about the game is crossing the ball for Don's first goal, doing my hamstring in the process and having to come off.'

One of the strengths of Swindon's rise had been, as every player you speak to from that era, John included, will testify to, the team spirit. The same players had been together for a long time; newcomers (as we have seen, perhaps too few of them) fitted in well. It was a good place to play football. That started to change at the end of April 1971 when the board, note the board and not the manager, signed Dave Mackay from Derby County to be player-coach for the following season.

On the face of it, it wasn't a bad move. Mackay was a great competitor and had a terrific record at both Tottenham and at Derby, where he had been instrumental in helping take the team into the First Division. The hope was that he would do the same at Swindon. The problem was not Mackay the player, it was the way the whole thing was done.

'We were in London because we'd just played at Queens Park Rangers, and we got back on the coach and the news broke that Swindon had signed Dave Mackay. I think everyone thought the same two things: firstly, surely he's not really coming here just as a player and, secondly, where is he going to play? We already had two good centre-halves in Frank and Stan.

It was very obvious that the board had done the deal because Fred seemed to be as much in the dark as anyone. He must have known that Mackay wouldn't be able to play for much longer, and then what was going to happen? I think the whole thing was handled badly. We got a player who, great player that he had been, was now well past his best, and we got a manager in waiting who unsettled the club. The story doing the rounds at the time, I don't know if it was true, was that one of the Swindon directors went to a game at Derby and ended up talking to one of their directors, and the conversation went round to what Derby were going to do with Dave Mackay as he came to the end of his career.'

Mackay made his debut for Swindon on the opening day of the 1971–72 season as the team lost 4–1 at Blackpool. So he could play in his preferred centre-back position, Stan Harland was moved to midfield. This didn't go down well with the captain, and before the calendar year was out he left the club, moving to Birmingham City.

'It was a terrible footballing decision to play Dave ahead of Stan. No disrespect to Dave, but he was no longer the player he was, and he was very slow now because he was getting on a bit and had a load of injuries, so it caused us problems as a back four. It meant we were all trying to cover him and eventually we couldn't do it. I personally didn't enjoy it because I was so busy covering that I couldn't get forward, which, as we know, was an important part of my game.

The other side was the fact that Stan had to play in midfield. Now Stan was a great centre-back, but no way was he a midfielder. So what it meant was that we had two players playing who shouldn't have been on the pitch in their positions – in key positions too. It's no wonder that we struggled.

The other person it affected was Roger Smart in front of me. Now I don't think Roger ever got the credit he deserved because he was a very fit fellow. I thought I was pretty fit, but I don't mind admitting that Roger was fitter than me. So Roger now has to cover me because I'm covering Dave. You can see that the whole balance of the side was affected.'

Initially Mackay's arrival seemed to have helped shore up the defence: despite that opening day hammering, just two goals were conceded in the next seven games. There was an undercurrent within the club, though, and when the side managed just one win in seven games between the end of September and the end of October, Fred Ford resigned, or at least officially he resigned, leaving the club after a 1–0 home defeat by Middlesbrough on 30 October.

'The writing had been on the wall since Dave arrived really, and I don't think Fred was ever happy about things after that. He was a good, hard-working fellow, Fred, and I think he deserved to be treated better by the club, effectively the board had decided to replace him once they signed Mackay. We were sorry to see him go, but all felt it was for the best because, although as a player you try and focus on your game and ignore any off-field politics, it was very evident that there were things going on behind the scenes.'

The rest of the season saw no real improvement. The team were never in any relegation danger but were never in the promotion picture either and ended up 11th, up one place from the previous season. The total of 47 League goals scored in the season was the lowest since the dark days of the 1950s. To put that in perspective, John had played in two seasons where the side had scored more than that total just in their home games.

'It was the start of my unhappiest spell at the club really. We went from a team that was doing very well, with good players who all worked for each other, to a much inferior team, where there just wasn't that same togetherness. The atmosphere at the club changed as well – I felt that some of the discipline went. Under Danny, the team almost ran itself because of some of the strong characters. Danny wasn't particularly strong as an organiser, but he didn't need to be because of the players he signed. Then Fred tightened things up – he was a good, organised coach. Under Dave I thought the training sessions were much too slap-happy – all we seemed to do was play five-a-sides and there didn't seem to be much thought as to what was being done or communicated to the players. It was poor really.'

The one break from a difficult League season came in the Cup – this time the FA Cup. The third round saw Arsenal drawn to play at the County Ground. A record 32,000 crowd turned up to see if the heroics at Wembley could be repeated, but, despite the presence in the Swindon starting line up of seven of the cup-winning side, Arsenal were too strong, winning 2–0.

'I'm afraid that there was never really any likelihood of us beating them again. They were still a good side, and we were fading fast. Although a number of the players were the same from our side as in 1969, a lot of the way of playing had gone, and I think, although it's a terrible thing to say, some of the spirit as well.'

Things were declining fast. The start to the following season, 1972–73, was poor, just four wins in the first 14 games. Mackay had stopped playing, and, although the regular back five contained four of the usual suspects (Downsborough, Thomas, Trollope and Burrows, with Ron Potter coming in for Mackay), there were clearly problems with the team. Things were equally bleak off the field with the club, burdened by interest payments on the new North Stand and hit by falling gates, apparently losing £150,000 a week.

'The simple truth was we weren't good enough. Some of the players who Dave brought in weren't up to the job and the togetherness, which counts for so much in football, just wasn't there. You could see and sense that we were on a decline. It was not a happy time.'

Something had to be done. The board's response to the financial position was to put the entire team up for sale. In reality, this was a signal that the board would listen to offers for the two players most likely to attract interest, Rod Thomas and Don Rogers.

There is little doubt that the board would have preferred to have sold Rod Thomas. Rogers was a Swindon institution, and he also, as a winger, had the advantage of bringing the crowds in, albeit to a lesser degree than before. However, no offers for the full-back were received, and on 28 October, after a 2–2 home draw with Brighton at the County Ground, Rogers was sold to Crystal Palace after 400 games for Swindon, all but a few with John Trollope behind him at left-back. After 10 years one of the longer-serving partnerships in Swindon's history was over.

'It's a long time to play with somebody, 10 years. You get to know their game, and they get to know yours, and very soon you find that you develop an understanding with them that is hard to replicate. I also got on well with Don off the field. He and Jane and Maureen and I used to regularly socialise together so, yes, him leaving was a big wrench. However, as a mate, I couldn't begrudge him going, it was a great chance for him to make his name for himself, and, in truth, I think he should have gone a few years earlier, perhaps in 1969 or 1970.'

Things now moved very quickly. The following Wednesday, 1 November, after exactly a year in charge, Dave Mackay resigned, leaving to join Nottingham Forest as manager. He would find limited success there, but would later replace Brian Clough at Derby County and take his old club to the First Division Championship (with Rod Thomas as part of that side).

'I hadn't realised he had gone as quickly as that after Donald. His appointment couldn't have been on the basis of what he achieved at Swindon could it? To be fair to Dave he did very well at Derby, but I have to say that he didn't do Swindon any favours whilst he was manager, and he certainly played his part in the decline of the club

– clearly not all his fault as money was tight, but he must take part of the blame.'

The new manager was appointed on 10 November 1972. He was Les Allen, part of the famous Allen footballing dynasty. His son, Clive, would later be a well-known goalscorer, particularly during his time at Tottenham. Allen senior had spent much of his career in London as a player with Chelsea, Spurs and Queens Park Rangers and then in management with the Loftus Road side.

'I never had any problem with Les Allen. He was a real gentleman. I did have a big problem though with his assistant, Gordon Eddlestone. Eddlestone came from Wolves as first-team coach and modelled himself on the then Wolves manager, Bill McGarry. I felt he treated us like kids. On occasions he'd leave us waiting outside in the freezing cold for 20 minutes or so for him to start training. He just wanted to play mind games with us to show who was boss. It didn't go down well with me, I can tell you.'

The season limped to a close. Twenty-two players were used, and, although there was a Cup triumph when First Division Birmingham City were beaten 2–0 at the County Ground in round three, there was little to cheer the fans. Gates slumped, just over 7,000 saw a 1–1 draw with Sunderland, an unthinkable decline for a team that had regularly been attracting over 15,000 to home games just a couple of years earlier.

After Rogers's departure, John had a new partner on the left flank. The flamboyant Tommy Jenkins was signed from Southampton, ostensibly to replace Rogers, but he was inconsistent and merely added to the sense that things were not 'how they had been.'

'I'm afraid Tommy Jenkins was an absolute nightmare to play behind. He was a good dribbler, but he just used to dribble across the pitch, so there was no end product. He didn't appear to have the footballing brain to bring other players into the game, and as far as I was concerned he basically stopped my overlapping because there was no point – he wasn't going to pass. I think initially the fans liked him because he could beat players, but there wasn't any end product – he wasn't a big goalscorer [four goals in 100 games was his final record] and he didn't create very much for others because he didn't link up with other players. In the end, the fans got as fed up with him as some of us did I think.'

You can sense John's hurt and disappointment even now, 30 years on, when he talks about some of the bleakest times of his career. Worse was to come. Towards the end of 1972–73, for the one and only time in his years at the club, he was dropped.

'I wasn't told I was being dropped, I was sat in the dressing room and the team was read out, and I wasn't in it! So I went upstairs to the Rendezvous Club, to get out of the way of those who were playing, and bumped into Cecil Green, one of the Directors, who just looked at me and said "what are you doing up here? You should be getting changed." When I told him that I'd been dropped he couldn't believe it.

Anyway, afterwards I went to ask why I was dropped and was told that it was because I "didn't hit enough long balls". I think that just summed up to me how bad things were becoming.'

Season 1973–74 is best forgotten. It was comfortably the worst season in all John's time at Swindon. Just seven games were won all season, and two of those were in the opening three matches, after which, ridiculously, in the light of what was to follow, the team were top of the table! The club was now in freefall. Twenty-seven players were used during the season. You would either need to be a fanatical follower of the club or have a very good memory to remember the likes of Richard Compton, Paul Fiocca, Mick McGovern, Chris Porter and Franco Sperti.

'No disrespect to some of those players, but they just weren't good enough. Some of them were locals who just had a brief spell in the League, and some were players that Les Allen signed. I remember he went back to Queens Park Rangers for a couple. Mick McGovern was one, and then there was a goalkeeper called Alan Spratley, who was never going to make it because he was too small. Then there was someone like Terry Hubbard, he was a good player but he was always injured – he just didn't have the body for professional football. I think some of Les Allen's judgement of players was flawed, and, of course, I didn't think much of the coaching we were getting from Gordon Eddlestone.'

Virtually all of John's old mates had now gone. This was the season that Rod Thomas departed for Derby County, leaving just Frank Burrows, Joe Butler and John as survivors from the side of the halcyon days. The problem was not just that the likes of Peter Noble, Peter Downsborough and Rod Thomas were going, it was that their replacements simply weren't good enough. Not only that, but for John personally things were going from bad to worse.

'The thing that annoyed me most then, and still does today, was the attitude of some of the senior players. When you are struggling you look to them to stand up and be counted, and that just didn't happen. One senior player used to regularly turn up for training drunk and nothing was done about that, whilst another, to put it bluntly, used to cheat us on the pitch during matches.

He used to start to make runs for you so you'd knock the ball there, but then he'd simply stop running or run the other way so it looked as if it was a poor ball. Worse still, he'd then play to the crowd and shrug his shoulders as if to say "what can you do with this lot?"'

The only good memory that John has of this season, easily his worst at the club, is of 19 January 1974. Not the game played that day itself, a 2–1 defeat at Sheffield Wednesday, but the fact that it was his 556th League appearance for the club, taking him past the record previously held by Maurice Owen.

'That was a big honour, of course, made all the better by the fact that it was Maurice's record that I was beating. Maurice had been my childhood hero, and so to first play with him and then to be able to overtake his record was a great thrill.'

Even a management change couldn't save things. On 28 February, two days after a home defeat by Luton Town (in front of 2,600 – the game was played on a Tuesday afternoon to save power during the three-day week), Les Allen was fired. Allen left with the worst record of any Swindon Town manager. While not all down to him, he had presided over the rapid decline of the club from Second Division mid-table to relegation fodder and few remember his time in Wilshire fondly – certainly not John.

'Off the pitch I had no problems with Les Allen, as I've said, he always treated people very well. However, on the pitch it was a terrible time. The players that he brought in just couldn't do the job. We were a very poor side, some of the players couldn't play and some just wouldn't.'

Allen's replacement was an old favourite, Danny Williams. The appointment, made on 6 March 1974, was, however, much too late to save the side from relegation, as they finished bottom, 10 points adrift of safety (a massive gap in the age of two points for a win) and with the lowest average gate in the Division.

'The game was up long before they brought Danny back, but at least it gave him some time to look at what he was inheriting and to begin to rebuild the club on the playing side ready for life back in Division Three. It says much for the state of the club that even Danny, with all his motivational skills, didn't really make much difference to the air of despondency around the club in his early months back.'

John's previous relegation had been close, and there was a sense that the club was in good shape. This time it emphatically was not.

BACK IN THE THIRD

By the start of the new season, 1974–75, John was 31 but had already set a new appearances record in League games for the club. He remained fit and well and, with his old manager Danny Williams, was at the helm. It was clear that he was going to be playing, injury permitting, for a while yet.

'Obviously, the big event had been going past Maurice Owen's record. At this stage I hadn't given any thought to breaking any other record. I just wanted to be playing regularly and to be enjoying my football, and with Danny coming back I was able to achieve that.'

The club had changed rapidly over a short period of time. New players were starting to establish themselves in the side. After the traumas of the 1973–74 season, the side had a more settled look and benefited from this stability to put in a much better season than many had expected.

'At the start of the season I don't think anyone was quite sure what to expect. We'd had a terrible 12 months, and you're never quite sure how much lasting damage had been done by that. Having said that, as a professional footballer you are usually confident in the summer – you look for all the positives because it's pointless starting a season thinking that you are going to struggle.

It was a while since we had played in the Third Division, and players were bedding down, so we were a bit of an unknown quantity really. But overall it turned out to be a good season.'

The side was buoyed by the goals of two players, striker Peter Eastoe, who had been signed from Wolves the previous season, and Witney-born winger Dave Moss, who had also made his debut the previous season.

Between them the pair contributed 40 League goals, but the fact that no other player could contribute more than three League goals was probably the reason why promotion was not achieved.

'I much preferred playing with Dave Moss to playing with Tommy Jenkins. Tommy was a great dribbler, as I've said, but rarely passed the ball. He couldn't reverse pass and bring me in on the overlap like Don Rogers had done. In fact, Les Allen used to tell me to stop making my runs up the wing because he said that I'd never be given the ball!

Dave Moss was different in that he was a good, two-footed player, who, although not in the same League as Don, was still a very aware footballer who brought me into the game. We worked well together, and it was good to go back to playing with someone who I could link up well with. It certainly made the game more interesting.

Peter Eastoe was a very good signing. He was a very good goalscorer. In fact, in my career I'd say he was one of the best that I played with. He had a superb spell that season where he couldn't stop scoring, and was a major reason why we did so well. We did get a bit dependent on him though, which may be one of the reasons why we didn't go up.'

John was playing in a new-look defence. In goal, Jim Barron had replaced Scottish youngster Jimmy Allan, John McLaughlin, a former Colchester United trainee, was right-back, while the regular central-defenders were John's long-serving colleague Frank Burrows and Colin Prophett, signed from Norwich after a successful loan spell. It took time to gel, as was witnessed in a 6–2 defeat at Crystal Palace.

'I remember the Palace defeat. We were hammered really. In fact, I think if I look back over my career I never did very well at London grounds. It was a time when we were trying to get used to playing together as a back five. Individually, I think we were all good players. Jim was an experienced professional who'd been around a while, John was a good, neat footballer who could pass well and Colin was a player in the mould of Stan Harland. The problem was that we didn't gel in the same way as the old back five of Downsborough, Thomas, Trollope, Burrows and Harland had.

We did start badly that year and in the end it was a factor in costing us promotion. It just took time for us to get used to playing together all over the pitch, not just at the back.'

In the end, the season followed a path that was all too regular during John's career. Swindon were excellent at home, taking 39 out of a possible 46 points at home, a truly outstanding record, but very indifferent away, where just three games were won: relegation, not promotion form.

'It was something that it's very difficult to explain really, and I suppose every manager is searching for the consistency that allows a team to play as well away as they do at home. Part of it was that we were always very confident at Swindon. Teams didn't like coming to play us, and we felt we would win our home games. The fans played a big part, attacking the Town End in the second half, we always thought we would score.'

For John personally, it was a welcome return to stability. After the problems of the Les Allen reign, he was restored to first choice left-back and played in all of the League games, the ninth time in his career that he had been an ever present in a League season. He also returned, briefly, to taking penalties, scoring twice from the spot in games where the regular penalty taker, Dave Moss, was injured.

'As I've said, I never minded taking penalties, although there was this thing at the club that our defenders shouldn't be the penalty takers, which was ridiculous when you consider how many defenders have done that job down the years. I think what happened this season was that with Dave out injured they asked for volunteers, and I was stupid enough to put my hand in the air.'

The main highlight though was once again an FA Cup run. Wins against Reading, non-League Maidstone United and Lincoln City saw Swindon through to the fourth round, where, once again (the fourth time in John's career that the two sides had been paired together in Cup competitions), they drew West Ham United. As in 1966–67, the tie saw the London side at home, and, as in 1966–67, Swindon achieved a credible draw at Upton Park. The replay saw nearly 27,000 crammed into the County Ground (never since, and, given current ground capacity, never again, have so many been in attendance there) to see Irish international Trevor Anderson give the home side a half-time lead, but the visitors equalised in the second half and a late winner by Trevor Brooking took them through, ultimately all the way to the Final and a triumph over Fulham.

'I think the Cup run showed how good a team we could be when we played to our potential really. We could easily have beaten West Ham at home, and they, as they proved when they won the Cup, were a very good First Division side.'

Another ever-present season for John followed in 1975–76, but, in direct contrast to the previous campaign, this was an awful year for the club. Widely tipped to win promotion, they won just five games before Christmas, and, although 1976 started better with a run of four wins in five games, a run of six defeats in nine games put them firmly back in trouble. In the end, relegation was only avoided by one point. Had the team not won at Aldershot on 14 April they, and not Aldershot, would have gone down. The final position of 19th in the Third Division was the lowest League position that John finished in during his career.

'That was an odd season really because there was no clear explanation as to why things went downhill. We had much the same players, and we had thought over the summer that we would have a very good chance of promotion. I suppose the start affected us more than it should have done and confidence suffered. I hadn't realised that we were so close to going down though. I do remember Will Dixon's goal at Aldershot as being critical at the time, but hadn't remembered just how critical in the context of staying up.'

Things were no better on the Cup front, if anything they were worse. Wins over Newport County, after a replay, and Hendon took Swindon into the third round where they were paired with non-League Tooting and Mitcham United at the County Ground. 2–0 up early on in the first half, Swindon appeared to be well on their way to round four, only for Tooting to equalise with two late goals to take the tie to a second game. The replay, at Sandy Lane, Tooting, was another of those low nights in Swindon's Cup history as the hosts won 2–1, much to John's displeasure.

'That was one of the lowest points of my career. You should never lose to a non-League club, even though they were a good non-League club. We should have won at Swindon, I do know that, but even then it was a shock to lose the replay. We all thought that we'd thrown away the game at Swindon, but we'd win the second game because they'd been a bit lucky to come back for the draw.'

John missed the first 11 games of 1976–77 after getting injured over the summer, much to the displeasure of his manager and the new coach, one Frank Burrows, who by now had nearly come to the end of his playing career and was embarking on what would be a successful coaching and managerial career.

'I injured my Achilles over the summer, out running round Highworth. I always enjoyed running, and was just out keeping fit when I felt a sharp pain behind my ankle and realised I'd done something to my Achilles. Danny and Frank were furious because it wasn't long before we were due back for pre-season training, and they thought there was no need for me to be doing extra running.'

John returned from this setback to play all the remaining 35 games as the team improved to finish 11th, once more hampered by an away record that saw just three games won. It was entertaining football though, as one might expect under the management of Danny Williams, with 68 goals scored (48 at home) and 75 goals conceded. The County Ground faithful, in particular, couldn't complain at the entertainment they saw. In 23 home League games there were a total of 81 goals.

Goals came from everywhere that season: Trevor Anderson and Dave Moss both scored 14 League goals, midfielder Ray McHale scored nine, and even centre-half Colin Prophet managed six goals. It was fun football, albeit not very consistent. As an example, in successive home matches they won 5–1 against York and lost 4–0 to Peterborough. They conceded four or more goals in League games on six occasions and scored four or more on five. It was like the old days.

'You certainly got your money's worth watching us then, typical

Danny really. It was what I would call 'off-the-cuff' football, very attacking, and I know the crowd enjoyed it. Sure, your fans want you to win, but I do believe they also want to be entertained as well, and we definitely did that. We were a good side, all over the pitch really, because that season we brought in Steve Aizelwood, who was a good footballing centre-half. In hindsight we probably played too much football and payed the price.

As I've said, the way we played reflected the approach of the manager, which is always the case to some extent. Danny was incredible in some ways in that he really did have the approach of 'let's just score more goals than they do'. You might think that when we were conceding all those goals he might get us doing more defensive work at training, but that was never the case. I'm not sure that would happen today. Most managers would have teams in for extra training and work on defending, I'm sure of it.'

It was also the season that John's old friend Don Rogers returned to the County Ground. It was a major event in the town, the return of the original local hero, but this wasn't the Don Rogers of 10, or even five, years previously. By now, the injuries that were to end Rogers's career at a comparatively young age were taking their toll, and for John, in some ways, it was quite sad.

'I knew Don had been having injury problems in London, but it wasn't until he came back and I saw him play that I realised how bad they were. He wasn't the same player. That great pace and ability to twist and turn had gone.'

The Cup provided, as it so often did during John's career, the talking point of the season. Wins over non-League sides Bromley and Hitchin went some way to exorcising the memory of the Tooting defeat and took Swindon through to a third-round tie at Fulham. Second Division mid-table the visitors may have been, but they had a couple of famous players: Rodney Marsh and George Best. It showed the potential of this developing Swindon side that after a 3–3 draw at Craven Cottage they cruised home in the replay, 5–0, a remarkable victory against a higher division side.

'I marked George Best – what a player he was. Even then, when he hadn't been playing regular football for the past three years or so, he was still very difficult to mark. You would close him down and think you had him covered, and then he would drop his shoulder or swivel and he was away from you. I'm glad to say that I played against him, but a bit relieved I didn't have to mark him when he was at his best, he was probably the best all-round player of my generation.'

The win over Fulham brought Everton to the County Ground in the fourth round, and brought back memories for John of an earlier fourth-round tie against the Merseyside club 14 years previously. On that occasion his side had been outclassed, but this time John played a full part in two tremendous Cup ties. The first game, which finished 2–2, will be best remembered for a wonderful equaliser from Kenny Stroud. The replay at Goodison Park brought only heartbreak as, after Trevor Anderson had given Swindon a second-half lead, the home side scored twice in the last 10 minutes.

'We did very well against Everton, who were a good side back then, and really could have knocked them out in either of the games. The game at Swindon saw that goal from Kenny Stroud that everyone remembers – you only hit one of those like that in your career. Up there we defended very well, and we were very annoyed about their winner because we thought Bruce Rioch had fouled in the build-up.'

The truth was though that Swindon were getting better, and Danny Williams was, once again, starting to build a side that could challenge for promotion. Like his sides of the 1965–66 and 1967–68 era, this team was not the finished article, but it was developing under the typical Williams formula: sign two or three key players each summer and build a promotion-challenging side in three or four years. John thinks this was Danny's great strength.

'I think Danny never got enough credit for the work he did in the mid and late 1970s, partly because he'd left before the team started to challenge seriously for promotion. Yet if you look at what he did second time round, he was laying down the foundations again, bringing through young players like Kenny Stroud and buying players like Roy Carter, Ray McHale, Andy Ford and Chris Kamara, who would be key players in the side under Bob Smith.'

John was 34 during the summer of 1977 as he began his 18th season as a professional footballer. By now his thoughts were starting to turn to the future.

'I'd started to coach locally by then at Garrards Athletic where I knew the team manager, and I'd already decided that I'd like to stay in the game when the time came for me to give up playing. I did my coaching badges that summer; funnily enough it was Fred Ford who was then a staff coach at the FA who took the course that I did.'

Season 1977–78, which was to be John's last full season as a professional footballer, was a comparatively uneventful season. The side moved up one place in the table to 10th. It was the usual story, solid enough at home with just four defeats but once more just four away wins. Cup interest was relatively minimal – a decent enough run to the fourth round of the League Cup was ended by Wrexham, then a Cup force in their own right, while Brian Clough's League Champions to be, Nottingham Forest, won an FA Cup third-round tie at their own City Ground to curtail a short-lived FA Cup run.

John played in 40 of the 46 matches, although he had, for the first time for many years, a real competitor for his place in Andy Ford, who had been signed in the summer from Gillingham and had been patiently waiting his chance by playing out of position at both centre-half and midfield.

It says much for John's fitness and ability that even at 34 he was still the first choice for most of the season; only towards the end of the season and injury did he lose his place, and then only briefly. However, by then he had made a very important decision.

'I was absolutely committed to going into coaching, and Danny knew that. Towards the end of the season, Frank Burrows left us to go to Portsmouth and decided to take the then youth coach at Swindon, Jack Smith, with him. This left a vacancy for the youth-team job and Danny decided to offer it to me.

The problem was that I still wanted to play. I still felt fit and in reasonable form, and I'd played for that season as a regular. Danny though, which I understand, forced me to make a choice by telling me that if I took the youth job I'd have to give up playing because I couldn't be a first-team regular and do the youth team justice. I thought about it for a while and decided to call it a day to get into coaching.'

John's 738th, and apparently last, League appearance for Swindon came on 3 May 1978 at Chesterfield, where he couldn't prevent a 3–1 defeat. After 18 seasons in the first team, his playing career was over, just 26 games short of the record of 764 League appearances held by Portsmouth's 'Gentleman Jim'.

'It was tempting to play on because of the record. Another half season and I would have been able to have got there. What I was keen to do, though, was to coach, and I couldn't be sure if there would be another chance like the one Danny was offering me. I'd had a good long career, shame about the record, but I'd just been lucky to get so close.'

But John wasn't able to retire as easy as all that…

THE RECORD

John's retirement from professional football started with a pleasant surprise. In the summer of 1978 he found out that he had been nominated for an MBE.

'I got a letter in June saying that I had been nominated for services to football. To this day I don't know who put me forward. Obviously I accepted. I saw it as an award not just for me but for the club as well. It was good recognition for a Third Division club.

I went up to Buckingham Palace in November 1978 to get the award with Maureen and the children, and we had a great day. It was the Queen herself giving out the awards that day, which isn't always the case, and she had been well briefed because she knew I'd played a lot of games, and she said to me "you've been at Swindon a long time, haven't you!" It was a great honour, and I consider myself very fortunate.'

John settled into the role of youth coach, now working under the management of Bobby Smith. The former Bury boss was an unknown quantity to John, but soon the two men formed a strong working relationship.

'Of all the managers I worked under, I would say that Bobby had the greatest interest in the youth team. He was always hugely supportive of what I was trying to do, and he made sure that the club saw the importance of the youth team by getting me to do a report every month to the board. Wilf Tranter was great as well, who was with Bobby, and the two of them created a good place to work.'

However, just two months into his spell as youth-team coach, John was given another job, the first-team right-back role.

'I'd still kept very fit, and Bobby had a problem at right-back because of an injury to John McLaughlin so he asked me if I was OK to play, and I found myself back in the first team, just a few months after I thought I'd played my last game. As I was right-footed, playing right-back wasn't too difficult, it was a little odd to start with after playing on the other side of the pitch for so long, but I got through the games alright.'

John played in three games at the end of September and beginning of October. Two of the games were lost. It had been a slow start and after 12 games just three had been won. There was little sign of the improvement that was to follow.

'It was a difficult start. There were a number of players who were settling in, and we took time to gel as a side. However, Bobby had inherited a strong nucleus from Danny, and over time he got it right.'

After those three games, McLaughlin returned, and John went back to coaching the youth team, convinced that his playing days were over. This was a youth team that had a number of players such as Charlie Henry, Kevin Badderley and Brian Hughes, who would later play for John in the first team.

'I think most coaches would tell you that they are really frustrated players, and I was no different really. I think I was pretty tough as a coach. I set high standards and expected the players to work hard and have the right attitude and was very hard on them if they didn't meet those expectations. To be fair, though, that first youth team I coached had some good characters and their attitude was spot on. That wasn't always the case in later years.'

However, there was to be more first-team football in another comeback. Regular right-back McLaughlin had been signed by Frank Burrows at Portsmouth and had left the club in December 1978, and his replacement was Bryan Hamilton, the former Northern Ireland international, who, although more famous for playing in midfield, took over the right-back role. Hamilton played in 10 games at right-back, and on his 11th game, at

Bobby Smith's old club, Bury, on 27 March there was a familiar face on the bench – John.

'It's crazy isn't it? To have a 35-year-old full-back on the bench who had officially retired! I'm not sure why I was named as substitute. Perhaps they thought Bryan was carrying an injury – it does seem very odd.'

John came on in that game for new striker Alan Mayes, recently signed from Watford, although he is sure that he didn't play up front when he came on, despite his experiences at Oldham in the 1960s. The following game, away at Gillingham, he was on the bench again, this time he came on for Hamilton and impressed Bobby Smith so much that he kept his place for the last 13 games of the season.

The season very nearly delivered a third promotion for John. After an uncertain start, the side started to improve. New players, such as striker Andy Rowland from Bobby Smith's old stomping ground at Bury and winger Ian Miller from Doncaster, joined an established side put together by Danny Williams to mount a serious promotion challenge. The signing of Alan Mayes in February was a masterstroke – the diminutive striker scored a hat-trick on his debut at Rotherham and went on to score 11 goals in 21 games.

'It was a good, developing side, and there were some parallels with the side of the late 1960s in that it had been pieced together over two or three years by Danny, and then Bobby had added in a couple of extra players like Alan Mayes and Andy Rowland. The team spirit was good, and they had a good couple of years together.'

In an eerie echo of the promotion season 10 years previously, one of the sides competing with Swindon were Watford, then in the early stages of their glory years under the leadership of manager Graham Taylor and chairman Elton John. As in 1969, there was a showdown at the County Ground towards the end of the season, this time on 16 April. This time it was the home side who won, in front of the Match of the Day cameras, by two goals to nil, and John had a major part to play in that.

'The second goal was one of the goals of the season on television. [It was scored by Andy Rowland with a volley from the edge of the area, after John had begun the move with a run and cross from the right.] Some years later the move was featured in a book, and I was asked to sign the page. There was a diagram about how to create a goal through crossing, movement and shooting. It was a good goal, there's no doubt about it, and it was nice to play a big part in it.'

After that win Swindon were favourites to go up. Only one point was taken from the next two games, both away, but then three successive wins meant that Swindon came to the final two games of the season knowing that two wins would see them Champions of Division Three, thus giving John, at the age of nearly 36, a chance to pick up the medal that he still feels the team from 1969 should have won. It wasn't to be. Both games, at Sheffield Wednesday (1–2) and Blackpool (2–5), were lost, and the team finished three points behind second-placed Watford in this era of two up and two down. The rest of the team would go on to another heartbreaking season the following year, but for John it was time to hang up his boots again.

'I can't remember much about the two games at the end of the season, apart from the disappointment of not going up, we'd had a great run and managed to get much closer than I think anyone at the club was expecting. It was always going to be difficult to win both games, and obviously once we lost at Sheffield we knew we were going to struggle to go up, so Blackpool was always going to be very tough. I'd enjoyed it though – playing in a good team, a successful team, and one that always tried to play good football. However, I was conscious that it was taking me away from the coaching side, and I needed to do that full-time so it was only ever a short-term solution while Bobby worked something out in the summer.'

The following season, 1979–80, saw John focused on his youth-team job. John Templeman was signed from Exeter City in the summer to take over as first-team right-back, and his services were, therefore, not needed in the first team, not that he was worried.

'I was happy to be back with the youth team, it's what I wanted to do, and I realised I had been fortunate to be given the job at Swindon and got into coaching without having to move clubs. I knew I was closer still to the record [at this stage he was just nine games away], but it would have been wrong for me, and for the club, for me to have stayed in simply to have got that record, and the truth is Bobby needed to get things sorted out for a more permanent solution.'

Meanwhile, John also kept an eye on what was happening at first-team level. It was an exciting time for the club, and for much of the season the side looked as if they might match the achievement of the 1969 side and win both the League Cup and promotion. In the end, neither was achieved. The League Cup run, which included another epic win over Arsenal (4–3 at the County Ground in a fifth-round replay), was brought to an end in the semi-final by Wolves, while the promotion challenge tailed away as the pressure of playing 17 games in the last two months of the season proved too great. There was also a decent run in the FA Cup, only ended with two late goals by Spurs in their fourth-round replay at White Hart Lane, after Swindon had led for much of the second half.

'I was involved that season, in that I was with the first team on the periphery. Bobby used to like his staff in the dressing room before matches, and I also sat on the bench for some of the games. I certainly saw most of the home games, and I was at Wolves for the second leg of the semi-final, when I thought we were on the wrong end of some bad decisions. There was some foul play by Wolves, Emlyn Hughes in particular as I recall. I thought the team were very unlucky, they were very good to watch and played good football. It just started to go wrong when Bobby tried to bring in some bigger name players, people like David Peach, that season, and then the others over the summer. They were on more money than the players who had been at the club for a while, and once that came out, as it always will do, it affected the team spirit.'

Hopes were high for the following season, 1980–81. The nucleus of the side had stayed together, including the two strikers Alan Mayes and Andy Rowland, who between them had scored 56 goals in the League and Cup during the previous season. Over the summer some of the money from the Cup runs had been spent to bring in full-back Colin Barrett from Nottingham Forest (then European Champions), goalkeeper Tom

McAllister from Blackpool and central-defender Andy Rollings from Brighton and Hove Albion (then in the First Division). They joined a couple of other big-money signings, who had joined the previous season but had only played after the Cup runs were over, midfielder Glenn Cockerill from Lincoln City and left-back David Peach from Southampton.

'I think we all thought we would do very well. We still had most of the players who had done so well the previous year, and Bobby had brought in some 'names' in the summer. However, with hindsight, they weren't good signings. None of them really performed for the side, and, as I said, the money they were on soon became an issue. I don't know why Bobby signed them because they didn't add anything to the side, and I suppose in the end they contributed to him leaving the club.'

In the event, the season got off to a terrible start, which led to significant repercussions for John. The first five matches were all lost, the new look defence conceding four goals at home to Fulham and away at Reading and three goals at Sheffield United. Something had to be done; Bobby Smith's response was to recall, at left-back, the 37-year-old John, who came back into the side for the home game with Rotherham United on 13 September, replacing David Peach.

'The day before the Rotherham game, I was in the bath and Bobby Smith came in and said, without warning, "I want you to play tomorrow". I was very shocked, I had no inkling that anything like that was on his mind, despite the poor start. I took some convincing, but Bobby was adamant, he felt he couldn't trust David Peach, and he was sure that I would be fine because I'd kept myself very fit. In the end, I agreed to play and I enjoyed it. I had no problems fitness wise, I'd had a few games for the reserves, and I felt I did alright against Rotherham, particularly as I was up against Tony Towner who was a very good winger on his day.'

John played his part in a mini-revival, three of the next four games were won with only three goals conceded in that time, as he lined up in a back four, in front of stalwart Scottish goalkeeper Jimmy Allan, that read Charlie Henry at right-back, Russell Lewis and Roy Carter in central-defence and

John at left-back. All four of the 'big name' signings – Barrett, Peach, McAllister and Rollings – had failed to last beyond the first month of the season in the first team. John was settling back in nicely into first-team football, but he was, like everybody else at the club, in for a big shock. On 30 September, despite the improved form, Bobby Smith, who had been the most successful Swindon manager for a decade, was unexpectedly sacked.

'I was extremely surprised, and to this day I still think the board were much too hasty in getting rid of Bobby. Yes we'd had a bad start but there was every evidence that we were turning things round, and Bobby had given the club two very good seasons in the two years before. He should have been given more time, and had the board been less hasty I am sure he would have gone on and given the club a decent season. I still don't know why he was sacked, but I guess the fact that his big name signings hadn't done well must have been a factor.'

The new manager, in a temporary capacity, was Danny Williams, back for this third spell as manager of the club. Williams had stayed at the club after giving up the first-team reigns in the summer of 1978 as general manager and chief scout, so it was an easy option for the board to turn to him.

'The board wanted stability and Danny was an obvious choice to turn to while they worked out what to do. It was good news for me, of course, because Danny was happy to keep me in the team!'

There was, sadly, no noticeable improvement when Williams took over. The problem, remarkably for a team that had scored well over 100 League and Cup goals the previous season, was putting the ball in the back of the net. After a 2–1 home defeat by Chester on 4 October they only scored two goals in the next four games, meaning that since the 4–3 home defeat by Fulham in August they had only scored eight goals in 12 games.

'I think there was a general lack of confidence in the team at that time. Everyone had been shocked by how poorly we had started, and the change of manager hadn't really made a difference to us in terms of form. You can't just blame the strikers. If you look at the statistics, Alan Mayes and Andy Rowland were still scoring, although less frequently, but not many other people were.'

For John, a very special record was drawing near. You will recall that on his second retirement at the end of the 1978–79 season his League appearances stood at 756, just eight short of the record. Now, unexpectedly, he found himself with every chance of breaking that record. Danny Williams was happy with his form and this was looking like a longer comeback than John had first envisaged.

'I was very pleased with the way it went, particularly considering I hadn't played for a year or so. My fitness helped, but generally it was my positional sense and understanding of the game that enabled me to play to a reasonable standard. Yes, my legs weren't as energetic as they once had been, but I was able to compensate for that.'

The big day eventually came round on 18 October 1980. John played left-back in the home League game against Carlisle United, in a game that finished 1–1. It was his 765th League game for his one and only club. The record for most League appearances for one club was his.

'There was a lot of media interest, of course, both national and local, and the papers arranged for me to meet up with Jimmy Dickinson who was really good about me breaking his record. I don't remember much about the game, probably by that stage of my career I was on auto-pilot.

Looking back, I think I do realise now, perhaps more than I did then, what an achievement it was. To be the player who has played the most League games for one club in the 120 years or so of League football is a big honour. I was lucky, of course, because I only had the one serious injury, and I was lucky to have a manager who gave me a debut at 17, and another one who was still prepared to pick me when I was 37. In fact, I was lucky that all the managers seemed happy with me as a player, all it would have needed was for one manager to decide they didn't rate me and there would have been no record.

Do I think the record will ever be broken? I don't know is the answer. I suspect that if someone does then it will be a goalkeeper. I just think that in this day of squad rotations and Bosman transfers it's less likely that a player will stay at a club for the near 20 years they would need to in order to break the record as an outfield player.'

John's playing career was now, finally, coming to an end. He played in the next five matches, but only one of them, a 4–3 win at Exeter City, was won. However, his playing career was over after a 1–0 defeat by Colchester United on 4 November. It was over, not through injury or poor form but because of one reason, he was going to be the new manager.

'I think when Danny took over as caretaker there may have been some thought that he might end up taking over again on a permanent basis. However, the results weren't going well and I don't think he was enjoying it very much. Anyway, at the beginning of November Danny pulled me to one side to say he thought that if he recommended me to the board they would offer me the job, and did I want it?

I have to say that I didn't really want the job. I didn't think I was cut out to be a manager, and I was enjoying coaching and, indeed, playing. In fact, if I hadn't taken the job I honestly think I could have kept on playing until I was 40. I was certainly fit enough to do so. It took me a long time to decide whether to accept or not. I remember John Nicholas, who was the club doctor and is still involved with the club even now, said to me not to take it. He told me that I didn't need the job and that sooner or later I, like most managers, would get the sack, and I would be better off staying as youth-team manager.

However, there were others who were telling me that I should take the job because I would regret it later if I turned it down. They felt that this was a big opportunity with 'my club', and I should test myself as a manager.

Anyway, in the end, after getting an assurance from the board that I could have my old job as youth-team coach back if things didn't work out, I took the job.

It was my worst decision in football.'

MANAGEMENT

John inherited a side struggling to maintain form. Most new managers do. In John's case, Swindon were looking as if, completely contrary to the promotion push everyone at the club (and indeed most football pundits) had been predicting, they would be locked in a battle to avoid relegation. Just four wins in their first 19 games had led to the management change, and the most recent form was shambles – just one win in the last 10.

Yet the team was essentially a good one, still the nucleus of the team that had gone so close to both promotion and Cup success the previous year. For his first game in charge, away at Blackpool on 15 November 1980, John could call on nine of the players who had played in the Cup semi-final the previous season, just Billy Tucker and Ray McHale being absent. The start of John's management career was a good one, the team getting a useful point at Bloomfield Road in a 1–1 draw.

'I'd taken the reserves before, so it wasn't a new experience to be in charge in the dressing room with some senior players, but it was difficult at first because I'd played with so many of the players – both that season and also earlier in my career. I felt I'd served a bit of an apprentice in the youth and reserve jobs but was conscious the opportunity to run a first team had come quite early really. It was a bit odd to start with, and I do know it felt strange at Blackpool to think that this was now 'my' team, although I can't remember much about the match itself.'

It is common practice in football that, in the short term initially, a change of manager will often bring about an improvement in results. Players tend to feel they are playing for their place and their future under a new man, everybody is keen to impress and the new manager's way of doing things can feel innovative and new.

So it was with John. Immediately after his appointment the side went six games without defeat and four wins, helping everybody to feel better about the way things were going, although there was defeat in the FA Cup second round at Fourth Division Wimbledon after a nervy home win over non-League Weymouth in round one.

'Early on it went very well. I thought that the players responded well and that the senior players in particular gave me more effort than perhaps they'd been doing earlier. That made for a happier ship, and as a result the performances on the pitch got better, and we started to make some good progress in the League.'

In that run two important changes happened. Firstly, on 29 November, for the home game with Hull City, John gave a debut to the England Schoolboy striker Paul Rideout. Rideout, scorer of one of the all-time great Wembley goals the previous summer in a schoolboys international against Scotland, came in for Andy Rowland and became, at the age of 16 years and 107 days, Swindon's youngest-ever player. He scored as well as the team won 3–1.

'I knew Paul well through my work with the youth team, and it was very obvious that he was going to be a very, very good player. He could have had the choice of any club really, but the fact that his mother was a Swindon girl helped us, and I think he liked the set up at Swindon as well. He was from the Southampton area, and all credit to our scout down there, Keith Williams, for his part in persuading Paul to come to us.

When Paul moved to Swindon his mum and dad came up too and ran the hostel the club had on Shrivenham Road for many years, and I got to know them very well. The fact that they were here helped Paul to settle, and, although he was a bit headstrong, he was very confident and physically very strong. He was a man at 16 really, so I had no hesitation in giving him his debut. He did very well, as you'd expect, and had a cracking goal disallowed as well as scoring one.

I suppose in the end Paul didn't really fulfil his potential. I, and many others, always thought that he would play for England, but he lost his way rather. The move from Swindon didn't help, he could have gone to Liverpool, which would have been a good move for him because they would have developed him and gently brought him into the first team, which was probably what he needed. Instead he went to Aston Villa, and although he went straight into the first team he was playing in an average side at that level and too much was expected of him.

The other thing that I noticed about Paul as he got older was that he didn't get in the six-yard box often enough, he tended to score some great goals from outside the box, but he didn't get many tap-ins, which would have boosted his goals tally and helped him perhaps get another big-money move to one of the top English clubs.

He was a super lad though, and I was proud, many years later, when his dad, Dave, told me that I'd had a big influence on Paul's development, both as youth-team coach and as his first manager as a professional player.'

Then, after the 3–1 home win against Walsall on 19 December, John had to part company with one of his stars, striker Alan Mayes, who went to Chelsea for £200,000. Even in a struggling side, Mayes had still managed 12 League and Cup goals, and his departure would be keenly felt.

'Alan was a good little player and would always score goals, but we had no choice but to sell him because of the financial position of the club. He lived near me in Highworth, and I remember going down to his house to tell him that the board had accepted a bid for him from Chelsea and that he would probably have to go. He took it very well. I think he knew that he was one of the club's big assets, and with the club needing money it was always likely that he'd be moving on.'

In the New Year, 1981, inconsistency was the problem. In January two out of three games were lost to put pressure back on the team at the wrong end of the table. February, however, was much better with three wins in the month, including a 5–2 thrashing of Sheffield United at the County Ground. Thereafter, although from March until the end of the season the team only lost three games in 13, only one was won, a 3–0 win against Colchester on 11 April when Rideout scored twice. A succession of draws kept Swindon in trouble, although John's ability to organise a defence was very evident – just 10 goals were conceded in the last 13 games of the season, indeed, under his management, the defence conceded just 23 goals in 27 games. It was that ability to keep the goals out (and keep clean sheets – six of the last 12 games were drawn 0-0) that eventually kept Swindon up – just. Safety was assured when they drew 0–0 at home to Brentford on 2 May . It had been very close.

'We did work very hard at the defensive side of our game, which I suppose you'd expect, given the position I played in. We just tried to stay up that season, it was always going to be a struggle given some of the off-field problems at the club, and I just felt that our best chance was to keep things tight in defence because it was clear that, before I took over, we had been conceding too many goals. The defence became more solid – Charlie Henry established himself at right-back, Russell Lewis became the first choice centre-half, and I brought back Kenny Stroud, who was still a good footballer even though he was coming to the end of his career, to play alongside Russell. It wasn't just the defence either. Chris Kamara and Roy Carter did a good job for me in front of the back four to keep things solid.

We were just relieved when the final whistle of the Brentford game went – it had been a long season, and although none of us had expected a relegation battle that's what had happened, and we were grateful to have survived.'

So what had John learned in his first six months of management?

'Initially I think it had gone well. The senior players were supportive and the youngsters who I brought in had done well. The dressing room seemed reasonably united, and we pulled through a difficult situation. I wasn't afraid to give out a few rollockings, although I was careful to do that more to the senior players because

I think you need to be careful with the youngsters as they're learning their trade. Perhaps the view of some of the senior players, who later felt I favoured the youngsters, was already sown, but because we generally did OK it didn't come out as much as later. But that first season I did enjoy it to a certain extent.'

For John's first full season in charge, 1981–82, he rang the changes in the playing staff. Out went some of the big-money signings from the previous regime: Andy Rollings and Colin Barrett. Stalwart midfielder Chris Kamara moved, briefly to Portsmouth and then on to Brentford, but he would return to the County Ground later, winger Ian Miller moved to Blackburn, midfielder Glenn Cockerill, who had never really settled at the County Ground, returned to Lincoln City and Brian Williams went to Bristol Rovers. That's a lot of experience out of the door.

'I was told to get rid of the high earners, simple as that. We paid some off and others we transferred, just to get them off the wage bill, and replaced them with younger, cheaper players. I lost some good players too, Chris Kamara and Ian Miller, and I had to swap Brian Williams to get Gary Emmanuel. Glenn Cockerill left as well, he'd been a huge disappointment – Bobby had signed him from Lincoln as one for the future, but I felt he didn't do the business for us, sometimes down to a lack of effort, he'd say it was because I didn't like him, which isn't true.'

There were some newcomers, a mixture of experience and youth. At one end of the scale was Ken Beamish. The 33-year-old striker, best known for his time at Blackburn Rovers, became assistant manager. This was John's choice.

'I have to be honest and say that my first choice as assistant manager was Billy Tucker, who'd played with us as centre-half. However, Billy wanted to stay in his job as an accountant and didn't want to move into football full time. I'd never met Ken in my life, although I knew of him because he'd been a long-serving player at Blackburn. Someone recommended him to me – I forget who – and I asked around and got a positive response so I decided to bring him in, and I felt we worked well together – in fact, I still see him from time to time when I'm at Preston with my job. He's commercial manager at Blackburn now and has put on quite a bit of weight!

Don Rogers came in as my youth-team coach and did a good job, so I was happy with my backroom team, although with hindsight, given it was my first job as a manager, perhaps I should have had someone more experienced than Ken as my assistant, someone who had been there and done it, particularly as we started to struggle.'

On the playing side, experience was provided by Gary Emmanuel. The 27-year-old midfielder joined from Bristol Rovers in a swap deal with Brian Williams. The other signings were younger: defender Mike Graham from Bolton Wanderers, striker Craig Moores, also from Bolton, winger Howard Pritchard from Bristol City and full-back/midfielder Gary Williams from Blackpool.

'I wanted to play with two men wide, and having lost Ian Miller and Brian Williams I needed two new players in that position, which is why I signed Gary Williams and Howard Pritchard. I though Craig Moores would do better than he did, but if you look at Mike Graham he stayed at the club for a while and did a good job in the centre of defence. The problem was money, though. Because we had to reduce the wage bill we were replacing senior professionals with people learning the game, and we were always taking a big gamble on those youngsters growing up very quickly.'

Season 1981–82 started well. Four goals were scored in each of the first two home matches, and the team were unbeaten in their first five matches with just two goals conceded, before local rivals Reading ended their unbeaten record with a 2–0 win at the County Ground on 26 September. The team against Reading gave some indication of John's approach to management. It included four players who had been in John's youth team: full-backs Charlie Henry and Kevin Badderley, both 19 (the youngest pair of full-backs at Swindon since John himself and Terry Wollen had made their debuts together in 1960), and central midfielder Brian Hughes, also 19.

'I'd like to say that it was all part of my grand plan to play all those young players, but that wouldn't be true really because it was more down to the financial position. Yes, I did believe in youth in that if the players were good enough then we should play them, but in an ideal world we would never have blooded so many at the same time, whilst they were good players they weren't in the league of the 'Bert's Babes' team. The problem was that we just couldn't afford to pay any sort of wages so experienced players wouldn't join us – the kids were on peanuts for professional footballers and that was keeping us financially afloat.'

The next game after the Reading defeat, at home to Chesterfield, also saw the side beaten, but three successive wins then took Swindon to the top of the table, much to everybody's surprise, including the manager's.

'No, I never thought we'd be top of the table, I was just hoping to develop a young side that might be able to challenge for promotion in a couple of years. However, early on we did play some good football, which pleased me because I always wanted us to do things in the right way on the pitch. We were scoring loads of goals, and the youngsters were doing very well.

We played well at Bristol Rovers. Any side that scores four times away from home in a game must be playing well. Terry Cooper, who was then the manager of Bristol Rovers, lost his job as a result of that win, which was unfortunate.'

That was the high point of the season. The first 10 games of the season had brought six wins, the remaining 36 would bring just seven wins as the side slid down the table. After that win at Bristol Rovers, the side wouldn't win again until the end of January. While a number of postponements meant that some of this was due to matches being called off, it was still an 11 game run in which just three points were gained. The defence, which had conceded just eight goals in the first 10 games, now leaked like the proverbial sieve – 25 goals in those 11 games.

'The game after the Bristol Rovers game was at Walsall and we lost 5–0, which just shows how inconsistent a young side can be – within four days we'd gone from a superb performance to a very poor one.

There were a number of reasons why we couldn't get out of the bad run once we were in it. The first one was the experience of the players. Their confidence started to go on the back of losing a number of games, and they didn't have the experience to turn things round. Secondly, you have to remember that I was a young manager, and I probably lacked some experience as well in that I wasn't always sure what to do. With hindsight, I also suffered from having an inexperienced number two in Ken Beamish. I know I'd appointed him, and he did a good job, but I might have been better bringing in someone who had done more time in management. Danny Williams was still at the club, but we needed some tactical input on some occasions, and Danny would be the first to admit that wasn't his strength.

We did need to freshen things up in terms of bringing in some new faces, particularly some experienced faces, but we just didn't have the money, even to bring someone in on loan, so we had to go on with what we had. It wasn't helped by what I felt was a lack of leadership among the senior players. When you have a young team you look to your older, more experienced players to lead you on the pitch, and I don't think that some of them did that.'

The run was ended with a home win over Exeter City on 31 January. This prompted a revival with just one of the next nine games being lost, although only two of these were won. The defence, at least, seemed more solid with just eight goals conceded in those nine games, as John again brought back his old teammate Kenny Stroud to play alongside Russell Lewis in the centre of defence and to bring extra experience to support his young full-backs. There was hope that the worst was over and that the team could regroup and push for a mid-table finish.

'As is so often the case, once we finally won a game some of the confidence started to return, and we went on a good little run, which gave us a bit of a chance of getting out of trouble. I think it shows that we weren't that bad a side when things were going reasonably well for us, it was just that consistency that we needed.'

However, problems were mounting up, both on and off the pitch. On the pitch a chronic shortage of goals now threatened the survival bid.

Between 12 March and 17 April Swindon played seven games. They only scored in one of them, a Paul Rideout effort in a 5–1 home defeat by Huddersfield, and only collected two points from a possible 21, which put them back in trouble. Off the pitch things were less than harmonious as well, with John again questioning the attitude of some of his senior players.

'I think that some of the senior players, as well as not taking the lead on the pitch, weren't totally for me, in fact I know they weren't because of some of the things that I've been told since. I know it was difficult for them because I'd played with a number of them, and it's always difficult to go from having someone as a teammate to having that same person as your boss, but I would have expected more from them as professional footballers. Not everybody likes the boss in football, but you should always do your best out on the pitch for the benefit of the supporters, who are paying your wages. I don't think some of the players in that side could say they were doing that.'

The run ended with a 3–0 win at Bristol City, themselves fighting to avoid relegation, and when the next two home matches were won, including a 3–2 win over another local side, Oxford, in a match which, symptomatic of the time, saw widespread crowd trouble both in and outside the County Ground, suddenly there was hope.

Three matches now remained, and because of the bad weather that had decimated the football programme over the winter two of those games were against the same team, Newport County. The first of the double header of games was at home, only a 1–1 draw was secured. Had the game been won, with the way other results went, Swindon would have been safe. That draw and a 3–0 defeat at Portsmouth in the penultimate game of the season meant that Swindon travelled to Somerton Park, Newport, on 18 May 1982 for the return fixture with the Welsh side knowing that they needed to win in order to stay in Division Three. Even now, nearly 25 years on, many Swindon fans still find it hard to forget that night. Swindon had chances. A Paul Rideout shot hit the post, but in the end they were beaten when Newport scored from a late penalty. Swindon were relegated to the Fourth Division for the first time in their history

'It was my worst night in football. I've got one record, which I'm very proud of, but I've also got another one, the only manager to take Swindon into the Fourth Division, which I'm not proud of at all, not that I can change it.

On the night it seemed to me that they wanted us to win. They were standing off and letting us shoot, but the truth is that even then we weren't good enough to be able to get the goals we needed. I think they would have been very happy for us to stay up because we were quite a local fixture to them, but it wasn't to be. It was a terrible night.'

So the club found themselves in Division Four. Not that the fans expected the stay to be anything but brief. After all, Swindon would now be one of the bigger clubs in the Division, with one of the best grounds. In fact, I can still remember a piece of graffiti scrawled at the 'Town End' around this era. It read, quite simply:

First Division Supporters
Second Division Ground
Third Division Team
Now playing in the Fourth

The fans may have expected much, but behind the scenes the situation was still desperate. The financial position was crippling. John was forced to let his old teammate Kenny Stroud leave on a free transfer – the club simply could not afford to match his previous season's wages. Roy Carter, another of the older heads, would also depart early in the season, which left John with a squad that only contained three players who could be described as anything like experienced: goalkeeper Jimmy Allan, midfielder Gary Emmanuel and striker Andy Rowland.

John might have wanted to bring in new faces, but money meant that there were only a couple, midfielders Paul Batty and Leigh Barnard.

'I really wanted to freshen things up a bit over the summer and to perhaps bring in a bit more experience, but not only was there no money for transfer fees but the wage budget was very low as well. I was lucky to get Leigh, he'd just been given a free transfer by

Portsmouth and was desperate to stay in League football so he was happy to sign for what were very low wages, even by Division Four standards. I thought he was a good signing, he served Swindon well long after I left and had a good career. He had a good engine, an excellent attitude to the game and did a good job for me on the left side of midfield.

Paul Batty was recommended to me by a contact in Doncaster and came down to play League football with us. Again, he did well for me, and I think you'll find he played over a hundred League games for the club. The other face who I brought in that season was Jimmy Quinn. He'd played a couple of times the previous season, but started to be more involved in this season, and, of course, he went on to have a very good career as well. I can't take any credit for finding him, he was recommended by one of my scouts. I think it might even have been Bert Head, who was doing some work for me at that time, who saw him play for Oswestry. We signed him for £2,000 plus a set of kit!'

You cannot accuse John of not trying his best for the club. He even came up with a novel way of raising money for the club.

'I was still pretty fit so I decided to run the Swindon Marathon in aid of the club that summer. It was hard work, particularly after 16 or so miles when I was out in West Swindon with not many people around, but I got round, and we raised a decent sum of money.'

The first half of the season went very well. After a slightly uncertain start, when two of the first four games were lost, including the shock of a 1–0 home defeat by Halifax, the side performed well. The next nine games saw six wins and three draws with six clean sheets, and after that run was ended by defeat at Darlington another run saw them win the next five games to put them second for the Christmas period. The financial position was no better, but at least the fans had a winning team to support.

'We started off very well, and, of course, the better the results the more confidence we got, particularly the younger players. We played some good football as well. We scored a number of threes and fours in the early part of that season, and I'd like to think that we kept the fans pretty well entertained. Up front Andy Rowland and Paul Rideout did well together. Rowland was good at holding the ball up, he led the line well, whilst Paul Rideout could win the game for you out of nothing.'

Then, inexplicably, things started to go wrong. A first home defeat since the Halifax game by Wimbledon, themselves going well, in front of over 8,000 during the Christmas period seemed to be just a slight knock back, particularly as Rideout was out injured. The next game was at Ashton Gate against Bristol City, and with the home side having a terrible time after being relegated with Swindon the previous season the promotion-chasing visitors would have expected to have won.

With a minute to go they were on course to do just that, but then a controversial equaliser for the home side changed that. Swindon claimed that the ball had been kicked out of goalkeeper Jimmy Allan's hands, Emmanuel was sent off for protesting too vigorously and two points were squandered.

After this, form was a little inconsistent, two home wins, during which a total of seven goals were scored, being sandwiched between two heavy defeats at Crewe and Port Vale. However, Swindon remained in a good position: sixth after the home win against Hereford on 12 February. Behind the scenes, however, things were not as good as they seemed.

'I think the pressure was really on because the expectations were there to go back up. The crowd didn't know about the financial position at the club, all they saw was a team in a Division that they considered it should never have been playing in. In a way I would have been better off if we'd started slowly, perhaps people might have then had less high expectations. Once we'd started so well there was a general feeling that there would be no problems for us to get promotion.'

That win over Hereford would be John's last as Swindon manager. The team now went on the run that would seal his fate and lead to him being asked to stand down as manager. The bare facts of the run are that the team lost six out of the next seven games. They were all close run things – only one defeat was by more than one goal – but it was a run that led the team to fade away out of the promotion race and proved to be the final straw for the fans.

'I don't think we played that badly in those games, it was just a run where things didn't quite go for us, and as a result perhaps a few of the young heads started to drop. The real problem for me was that the crowd started to turn against me, and once that happened it was going to take a brave board of directors to keep me on, and I didn't have that.

Of course, I think I would have turned it round, it was just a bad run, and the problem with people in football is that they tend to panic too much after a poor run of results. You only have to look at some of the managers who have lost their jobs in this last season (2004–05) after runs of say six or seven games without a win, which is nothing really. I mean, take Sir Alex Ferguson or Dario Gradi, in their different ways two of the great managers, their sides have had bad runs and their boards have backed them and reaped the reward.'

The end for John came after a home defeat by Darlington on 19 March. On the Monday the board asked him to stand down as manager. After nearly two years in charge his spell as manager was over.

'Some things stick in your mind over your career, and I will never forget one of the goals we conceded against Darlington. Jimmy Allan punched it into his own net. That summed it up for me really, I mean Jimmy was a top bloke, a very good goalkeeper, and had done very well for me when I was manager, and for him to make a mistake like that perhaps indicated it wasn't meant to be.

I could see it coming, particularly as the crowd was very unhappy that day, so I wasn't surprised to be asked to stand down. Part of me was a bit relieved, although of course I was also very disappointed that it hadn't worked out.'

So John left to be replaced by his assistant, Ken Beamish, initially on a temporary basis but eventually in a full-time capacity. His final record of 120 games in charge shows a virtually level record: 43 wins, 33 draws and

44 defeats. Considering the financial pressures he operated under throughout his time in the managerial position, it's a perfectly respectable record. So what are John's reflections on management?

'I wish I hadn't done it! I didn't really enjoy dealing with senior players, I found having to keep them happy just too difficult, and it took away from developing players, which is what I preferred. I don't think I did badly given the financial position I worked under, and I think I brought through and developed some players who went on to have good careers in the game, either at Swindon or elsewhere. But it wasn't really me. When Lou Macari took over at Swindon I remember him telling me that everyone in football has a niche and that mine was developing players, and I think he was absolutely right.

With hindsight, I wished I'd carried on playing when I stopped to do the youth-team job at 35. As I've said, I was fit enough to keep on going, and, although my legs would have started to have gone the older I got, my positional play and experience would have kept me out of trouble most of the time.'

So John was out of one job, but he would be staying at the club as a result of a clause he had inserted in his contract when he became manager.

'Because I was always so unsure about being manager, I got an agreement that if, or perhaps when, I got the sack as first-team manager I could return to being youth-team coach, and the club honoured that clause. I came in on the Monday as the first-team manager and left as the youth-team coach, there was no break at all. Don [Rogers] was the youth-team manager, and he had to make way for me, but there was no problem there. Don was hired knowing that would happen if I lost my job, and he had other business interests anyway so he was fine about it.'

The season limped to a close. In the end the side finished eighth, Ken Beamish doing enough to earn himself a full-time contract as manager for the following season, 1983–84.

That season would be Swindon's nadir. A season of almost universal poor football, in front of crowds which dipped below 2,000 for the last three home League games and saw the club at a new low. It was a difficult season for football generally, gates everywhere were down, as witnessed by the fact that the team played in front of just 880 at Chester, 1,008 at Halifax, 1,091 at Darlington, 1,214 at Bury, 1,274 at Hartlepool and 1,297 at Rochdale. It was the worst season in the club's history, and Beamish was unable to turn things round, hampered by the same financial problems as John had worked under. The team finished 17th, the only bright spot being an unexpected FA Cup run that took them to the fourth round

'Ken had the same problems as I'd had with money, there was just nothing to play around with. I kept a low profile working with the kids, and I don't think Ken found it a problem having me still on the staff, although you'd have to ask him that. It was a difficult time for the club though, and I don't think anybody involved enjoyed that year.'

At the end of the season Beamish was relieved of his duties. The club was at a low ebb and needed something to reignite it. That something would be a new manager.

ALL ABOARD THE SWINDON ROLLER-COASTER

Sadly, the definitive history of Swindon Town, *The Robins*, by Dick Mattick, only covers the club up until the end of the 1988–89 season, although Mattick did later produce an addendum to cover the extraordinary events of the start of the following decade. Should Mattick, the much respected club historian, ever produce an updated version of the club, or indeed should anyone else attempt to chronicle the history of the club, it is a fair bet that there would be a great deal of focus on the years 1984–93.

Put simply, it was an extraordinary period for a club who, up until that point, had been quietly plying their trade in the lower reaches of English football. Sure, there had been a couple of promotions, and, of course, the epic League Cup win, but generally there had been little for fans to cheer. All that changed as the club, under three high-profile managers, underwent an (all too brief) transformation from a struggling lower League side to one widely acknowledged as one of the best footballing teams in the country. John saw it all, as his beloved club changed beyond all recognition.

It all started in the summer of 1984 when the sponsors, Lowndes Lambert, decided to make money available to appoint a well-known manager. The financial situation at the club remained critical. It was only the intervention of the insurance group that enabled the board to appoint the man who would turn Swindon round, Lou Macari.

Macari joined from Manchester United as player-manager, having been a high-profile name in the game since his days at Glasgow Celtic in the

1970s. It stimulated interest in the club, and for John it was a major turning point in the history of the club

'Lou was an inspired appointment, and the board deserve a lot of credit for selecting him. Straight away things changed. Lou brought a real buzz and energy to the club, and indeed to the town, which hadn't been there for a while. I enjoyed working with him, and he started the recovery in the club's fortunes, which others then built on.'

Early on things weren't that promising. It took time for the new manager to settle in, and the team even suffered the ignominy of a home defeat by non-League Dagenham in an FA Cup first-round replay. However, gradually things improved and a strong run at the end of the season enabled the team to finish in a slightly flattering eighth position.

'I think Lou took time to find his feet. He hadn't managed before, and although he was clear on the way that he wanted the team to play he needed some time to sort out some of the playing staff that he had inherited. However, we gradually got better, and the players got fitter, which was a big focus for Lou, and you could see that we were building up a head of steam as the season came to an end.'

The big story of the season, however, was the sacking, and subsequent reinstatement of Macari over Easter 1985. The manager, recognising his inexperience, had appointed an older man as his assistant, Harry Gregg, who was known to Macari through Manchester United. However, the relationship between the two men soon deteriorated to the point where they were no longer speaking, which led to the board deciding that they had seen enough and sacking both men. This, in turn, led to a great wave of public support for the popular Macari, and after numerous protests by the fans the board relented, and Macari was reinstated, which, given what he subsequently achieved, seems to have been a wise choice.

John was in the middle of this. As youth-team manager he was part of the club's management staff, and he is well placed to comment on the rift that developed between manager and assistant manager.

'I have to say that I found Harry Gregg a funny fellow. I didn't find him very easy to get on with at all. In the end Lou got fed up because Harry was always disagreeing with Lou about how things should be done, in public as well as in private, and the relationship between the two just went very sour. I'm not sure why Lou didn't just get rid of him. It was just lucky for Swindon that the board were prepared to back Lou after they had sacked him because it would have been a terrible waste had he left the club for good.'

Gregg's departure opened the door for another role for John. To his surprise, Macari asked him to become assistant manager.

'I was very flattered to be asked because it was a sign of Lou's trust in me, after what he had been through, that he would give me the job. I know he asked around football and in the club about what I was like, and he must have liked what he heard! I did have to think about it for a while because I felt that I was happiest working with younger players, but I decided to give it a go, and I was very glad I did because we had some great times.'

The phrase 'great times', so often reflective of hyperbole, is accurate in this case. The following season, 1985–86, Swindon, with John as assistant to Macari, dominated the Fourth Division, accumulating a then League record of 102 points, despite having been as low as 21st in the League after a defeat at Hartlepool at the end of September.

'Once we got going there was no stopping us. Lou was very clear on how he wanted us to play, and because the players did some running every day they were incredibly fit. You would get to the last 20 minutes of a game and think that if you were level you would win because you would be able to outrun the opposition towards the end. We had some great successes. Colin Gordon was a good signing and that was the season that we played Charlie Henry up front, and he scored a lot of goals for us.

Whilst we had great success, I did find the way we played football wasn't how I wanted, lots of long balls relying on knock-downs and winning the second ball. However, it was effective, you cannot argue with results, and Lou used to say to me, when I expressed concerns about the style, that it was "horses for courses", ie play the system that suits your players. I think he was right early on, but I did think that towards the end of his time at Swindon, when perhaps he had better players, he could have given them more freedom. It's interesting that the team, which won the play-offs under Ossie, and played wonderful one touch football, was the same side as the team Lou had the previous year, perhaps the players were better footballers than Lou gave them credit for.'

The following season, 1986–87, was another successful season. Swindon were promoted again, this time through the play-offs, two Steve White goals bringing a 2–0 win over Gillingham in the deciding third game at Selhurst Park. It was an achievement that John is still proud of.

'We did very well that season. Obviously confidence was very high after the way we had won the Fourth Division, but any club that gets back to back promotions deserves a lot of credit. Again though, the secret was in the way we played and in our fitness – there was no debate about how we would play – everyone in the team knew the tactics, and we had the players, both in that season and over Lou's time at Swindon, to make the style of play work.'

At the end of that season John returned back to his youth-team role as Macari brought in Chic Bates to be his assistant. It was a move that had John's full support.

'Whilst I enjoyed my time as assistant manager, I did find dealing with the senior players harder than dealing with the younger players. They want more, they are more demanding and they can undermine you if you've got some strong personalities. I've said about Lou telling me that my niche was in developing players rather than managing them, and I'm sure that is right. I was happy to go back to the youth team, in truth I'd never been away because I'd still been involved with them, and done both the assistant manager job and the youth job with Terry Wollen helping me enormously with the youngsters. Chic and I shared the duties of assistant manager towards the end of that season, and then he took over in the summer, which was fine by me.'

Macari had two seasons with Swindon in the Second Division. A mid-table finish the first season was followed by a real promotion push in the second, as the club came as close as John's 1970 side had done to a first-ever appearance in the top flight of English football, losing only to Crystal Palace in the play-offs. After winning the home leg of the semi-final 1–0, they were beaten 2–0 in London in the second leg. John can look back fondly on some of the players who played in that era.

'I thought we had some good players in that era, some good, honest professionals who knew the game and played it the way that Lou wanted. Lou placed a lot of emphasis on his midfielders being box-to-box players, and we had a number of those, Lou tended to collect them, people like Steve Berry, Alan McLoughlin, Leigh Barnard, Mark Jones, who would have had a very good career had he not had serious knee problems, and, of course, Chris Kamara, who is now a regular on Sky. I must admit that I felt that Kamara just ran around a bit too much, although he was a good player he tended to be a bit like a headless chicken sometimes on the pitch in his enthusiasm. He always had a lot to say for himself in the dressing room as well, so I suppose it's no surprise that he's ended up in the media.

I think one or two players underachieved. I thought Phil King had the makings of a really top-quality left-back, but he used to suffer from a lack of confidence. He used to always ask whether he was up against a winger because he used to hate people running at him, which was crazy really because he was very, very quick. He didn't enjoy his training much either, and although he went on to play in the First Division with Sheffield Wednesday I think he could have played at the very top if he'd looked after himself more and had more confidence. I thought Jon Gittens was a bit underrated as well. He wasn't the best on the ball, but he was very quick, and with the full-backs tending to play quite a way up the pitch he had a lot of ground to cover.

Up front we had a number of players in that era. Jimmy Quinn, who I signed the first time round, served the club well. He held the ball up well and had the ability to drift out on to the left wing, which used to worry defenders and draw them out of position. Dave

Bamber was another who played in that era, again tall and gangly, perhaps not the best work rate, but able to win balls in the air for you and able to link up the play well.

Steve White was a real crowd favourite because he would always give everything. If he had taken a higher proportion of his chances then he would have played in the top flight because he got into great goalscoring positions. However, I think the best striker of that era was Duncan Shearer. I thought he was a class act – good technique both in and out of the box, and his goalscoring record spoke for itself when he was at Swindon. We should never have sold him.

The other thing about Duncan was he was always prepared to help the youngsters. I remember once I was coaching some of the young strikers at the old Wills training ground and encouraging them to make sure they were in the box all the time. Duncan walked past and obviously overheard what I was saying because he stopped and took 20 minutes with them to explain why being in the box was so important and how to make the most of your chances. He didn't need to do that, and the impact on the kids of a senior professional taking time out to talk with them and help them improve was huge.'

At the end of the 1988–89 season Macari's stock within the game as a manager was very high. He'd had five seasons at Swindon, during which he'd taken them from being a lowly Fourth Division side to the cusp of top-flight football. Unsurprisingly, he was in great demand, and that summer he moved on. John was expecting him to leave, but he was a little puzzled by the club that he left Swindon for, West Ham United.

'I think we were expecting Lou to go, he was a very high-profile and obviously very talented young manager, and he was going to be in demand elsewhere. I think he may also have felt, as I did as well, that perhaps the board at that time didn't really have his ambition. Lou wanted Swindon to be a First Division club, and I'm not sure the board did. I felt they were happy with being a good Second Division club, perhaps less pressure, I don't know.

I didn't expect him to go to West Ham, though. To me there were two sides at that time that always played football in a very pure way: Liverpool, with their pass and move philosophy, and West Ham, who had the reputation for being the academy of football with the way they approached the game. Immediately then you think something has got to change. Either West Ham are going to need to rethink how they approach the game or Lou is going to have to modify his style of playing. I just don't think it worked out for him, you heard rumours of senior players rebelling against the way he wanted to do things, which was sad really.

Lou did a great deal for Swindon and was really responsible for turning the club round. I enjoyed working with him, although our philosophy on football was very different. The only thing I would say, from my youth-team position, was that Lou tended to buy in players rather than bring youngsters in – not many of my kids got a run in the first team. I'm not sure at that stage that there were many who would have been first-team material, but perhaps there were a few who could have been given their chance. It wasn't until after Lou had gone that the likes of Fitzroy Simpson broke into the first team.'

Having struck gold with one high profile player-manager, the board decided to try again. This time the recruit was another international footballer trying his hand at management for the first time, the Argentinian World Cup winner Ossie Ardiles, forever immortalised in Chas and Dave's 1981 Cup Final song *Ossie's Dream*, which included the immortal line from Ardiles of 'win the Cup for Tottingham' sung in a heavy English accent. Like Macari's appointment, it came out of the blue.

'We had no idea who it was going to be, and it was a shock when Ossie was appointed because nobody at the club really knew him. However, he was great, particularly for me as a youth coach, because he encouraged everyone at the club to play a pass and move game, which I think is very beneficial for youngsters at their stage of development because it forces them to focus on the basics. He was the antithesis of Lou when it came to training though, it was the easiest physical training I've ever seen in my career, if it got too hot Ossie would simply cancel training!'

The players responded very positively to the new manager, and for the second season running they made the play-offs. This time they were successful, beating Blackburn in the semi-finals and then Sunderland in the Final at Wembley. It was an emotional return to the 'Twin Towers' for John.

'Being involved with a club like Swindon, you don't really expect to be going to Wembley at all, so having been there on three occasions is remarkable really. I certainly never thought I'd go back after 1969, but it was another great day against Sunderland. I thought the team played very well, and we should have won by much more than the one goal, we missed so many chances. I sat on the bench with the rest of the backroom staff, and although I wasn't directly involved with the first team at that time I still felt part of the win.'

So, after 109 years of existence, Swindon Town were now a First Division club, or at least they were for nine days. While the team had been performing so well on the pitch, there had been a shadow off the pitch in the form of an investigation into alleged illegal payments to players. It seemed very likely that the club would be found guilty of this charge, which related to events that happened during the Macari era at Swindon, and the question was always going to be what punishment the club would face. On 7 June 1990 they found out. They were relegated two divisions, from their proud position in the First Division to Division Three. It was a huge blow to everyone at the club. Nobody had foreseen such a draconian response by the Football League.

Although the club were subsequently reinstated back into the Second Division on appeal, the damage was done. That hard earned place in the top Division had been taken away from them. Even now, 15 years on, John is still bitter at how his team were treated.

'I thought it was outrageous then, and I still think that today. The problem for us was that they wanted to make an example of somebody, and because Swindon weren't a particularly big club and didn't have the political clout within the game that others would have had, the League decided to really hit us hard. Yes, we'd done wrong and should have been punished, but look at what happened afterwards. Spurs got a small number of points deducted and even got themselves back into the FA Cup when they were found guilty of the same thing, and, more recently, Chesterfield had a point deduction that didn't stop them getting promoted. So why were Swindon relegated two divisions? I know it doesn't excuse what we did, but everyone knows that what we were doing happens in football, in fact probably at most clubs in some way or another, so it seemed very unfair that we were treated as we were.'

At this point I have to broach a difficult subject: how much, as a member of staff, was John aware of what was going on? The question leads to a very open chat about what was happening. Indeed, John was more involved than he had realised.

'There were rumours at the club that the Inland Revenue might be investigating us, but nevertheless it was still a shock when a whole load of people turned up at the club one morning unannounced. Three people – two blokes and a woman – came to my office and went through everything. They questioned me for five hours.

The two main areas they wanted to question me on were about petty cash and man of the match awards to the first team. They brought in a huge pile of petty cash slips, which I was supposed to have signed to get money for the youth team, and when I say huge, it was a very, very big pile. They asked me for samples of my signature, which I gave, and that's where the problems started, because I always sign differently on official documents from if I'm signing an autograph. As we went through that pile of slips, I had to tell the investigators that none of them had been signed by me – it was someone impersonating my signature to get the money to pay the cash to the players. I know that others had their signatures forged as well, but obviously I can only comment on my own position.

The other thing they wanted to question me about was the man of the match awards that used to be given out. At the end of the game Lou used to hand out a brown envelope containing cash to the player he selected as a bonus. However, I knew something wasn't quite right because on occasions when Lou had been away and I had taken the first team he had given me the envelope before the game for the man of the match, and then told me who should get the award before a ball had been kicked. Of course, I knew there was something going on when this happened, but as I rarely took the first team I didn't do it very often, and I just assumed that the club owed that player money.'

It was a very difficult time for John. The Revenue had found some of the evidence they were looking for, and he now became a key witness. It would get worse. The case against the chairman, Brian Hiller, and the former manager, Lou Macari, would end up going to court at Winchester, and John was called by the prosecution to give evidence against the duo based on what he had told the investigators.

'It was one of the worst moments of my life. I went to Winchester Court, and when I was called I walked straight from a room behind a door outside the court and into the witness box, and there in front of me were my former chairman and manager. I had no choice though, I had to say what I had told the investigators, but it wasn't an experience I enjoyed at all, giving testimony against people you've worked closely with was very difficult.'

With all this happening, it is perhaps not surprising that the team struggled during the following season, 1990–91. They never really got going after an indifferent start and became embroiled in a relegation battle. To make matters worse, they lost their manager. Ossie Ardiles resigned in March 1991 to take over at Newcastle United

'Again I wasn't surprised when Ossie left. It must have been very difficult for him coming into the club and doing such a great job on the pitch, but having that affected by things that had gone on before he had arrived. Like Lou, he had built a good profile as a successful young manager, and there were always going to be clubs who would want to attract him, and I think the lure of a bigger club, especially as we were struggling, was just too great.

Ossie was better than Lou from a youth-team manager's point of view because he did let some of the kids have their chance. Fitzroy Simpson started to play regularly, and players like Nicky Summerbee, Paul Hunt and Adie Viveash also made their debuts. Of those, I though 'Oggi' Hunt had possibly the best potential as a kid, but he wasted it because of a combination of injury and his lifestyle off the pitch.'

By now the board at Swindon felt they had a winning formula: appoint an untried player-manager and wait for success to happen. It was no surprise, therefore, that they went, once again, for that type of leader, and no surprise that it was a well-known name, although few Swindon fans can have expected someone quite as high profile as Glenn Hoddle.

Hoddle joined Swindon from A.S Monaco where he had developed an interest in coaching while working under a young Arsene Wenger. He brought with him new ideas on everything from diet to when to breathe during training exercises and was another inspired appointment. Part of the reason for his success was the fact that he was a hugely gifted tactician, capable of reading a game from either the pitch or the dugout, but the other major reason was that he was still, even after injury and at the age of 33, capable of playing the game at a sublime level. For two seasons Swindon fans had the opportunity to see one of the most naturally gifted players England has produced in a sweeper role, displaying a range of passing not seen at the County Ground before or since.

'Glenn had a big impact on me because he had some new ideas. I'd not played 3–5–2 with a sweeper before, but once Glenn started to have the first team working in that formation he wanted every team in the club to play the same way, so I followed it as well. I thought it was a great way to play, it gave people the chance to express themselves on the pitch, and I am still a fan of it today.

We were lucky to be able to see Glenn on the pitch. He was just a superb footballer and a joy to watch. Yes, he was a good manager, particularly tactically, but don't underestimate how much influence he had on the team's performances and results because of his on the field contribution.'

Once Hoddle had kept Swindon up in the last few weeks of the 1990–91 season, he set about putting his stamp on the side. New players joined, most notably in midfield where Mickey Hazard and John Moncur, two excellent ball-playing footballers, joined, Moncur direct from Hoddle's old club, Spurs, and Hazard, with whom Hoddle had played at the White Hart Lane club, from Portsmouth. Once again, the quality of football was outstanding, with Swindon winning widespread praise from neutrals for the way they played the game.

Hoddle's first full season saw the club narrowly miss out on the play-offs. They would surely have made it had the club not been forced to sell top scorer Duncan Shearer for financial reasons in March. To this day, suspicions abound that the club who signed him, Blackburn Rovers, then managed by Kenny Dalglish, wanted Shearer not because they though he would play a huge amount for them but because they thought it would put a big dent in the promotion push of a club they feared. Regardless of whether this was the thinking or not, this is what happened. Shearer soon moved on from Blackburn, and Swindon, without him, just missed out on joining Blackburn in the play-offs, which the Lancashire side won to reach the Premiership.

The following season 1992–93, though, was a different story. For the third time in five seasons the team reached the play-offs (now the First Division play-offs after the introduction of the Premiership that season). Tranmere were beaten in the semi-finals, and then, on a dramatic day at Wembley, promotion to the Premiership was achieved, after one of the most dramatic games ever seen at the old stadium – Swindon Town 4 Leicester City 3.

'Glenn's footballing philosophy was a nice balance between that of Ossie and Lou, he was quite prepared to play the long ball if it was needed, but he liked his side to retain possession and pass. He was the mainstay of that side, they relied a lot on his distribution of the ball to the full-backs from the sweeper position. We scored a lot of goals that season playing the way we did. Paul Bodin did very well from left-back, and up front Craig Maskell and Dave Mitchell scored regularly, especially Maskell, who I thought was a very good goalscorer at that level.

Nobody will ever forget Wembley and the game against Leicester. Like Ossie, Glenn kept all his backroom staff involved, so I was on the bench that afternoon. What a game! I think the problem was that subconsciously the players may have felt that at 3–0 up the game was won and they relaxed a bit, which led to them being perhaps half a yard slower to the ball, and Leicester took full advantage. At 3–3 the impetus was definitely with them, and we were worried on the bench about how things were going, but fortunately we stabilised things after they made it 3–3 and went on to win, thanks to Paul Bodin's penalty.

I'm not sure now that I'll ever go back to Wembley in a working capacity, so I'm very happy to say that I have a record of three wins out of three there. I just consider myself fortunate to have been involved in one win there, let alone three, just think how many great players never experience that feeling.'

This time there were no off-pitch shadows casting doubt on the legitimacy of the promotion. Swindon Town were in the top flight of English football. The following season the humble County Ground really would host the likes of Manchester United, Arsenal and Liverpool.

There was, however, one fairly large cloud on the horizon. As with Macari and Ardiles, Hoddle's success had not gone unnoticed by the top clubs. Even before the play-offs there were rumours of Hoddle leaving. By the time of the traditional open-topped bus round Swindon to celebrate the promotion, it was an open secret that Chelsea was his likely destination. Thousands of supporters held placards given out by the local paper, *The Evening Advertiser,* pleading with the manager to stay, but it was to no avail, Hoddle left, and for the third time in four years the club needed a new manager.

'I think we all knew that Glenn would go, once the approach from Chelsea had become public. He was ambitious to succeed as a manager, and probably felt that he had done his duty to Swindon by getting us into the Premiership, which nobody could have dreamed of when he was appointed. It was a huge loss though, because it meant that we lost not just his managerial acumen and his experience of the top flight but also his ability as a player. He was still our best player then, even though he was well into his thirties. Would we have stayed up if he'd not left the club? Yes, I think we might well have done. In the end we just had too many people who were inexperienced at the top level of the game, from the manager down to the players, to survive, and by the time we found our feet we were as good as down.'

Originally, Hoddle's assistant, John Gorman, had decided to leave the club with his good friend. The pair would go on to be an established managerial double act wherever Hoddle managed over the next few years. However, in a desperate bid to try and make sure there was some form of continuity, the board tried to keep Gorman by offering him the manager's job. He accepted and brought in Andy Rowland as his assistant.

John is clearly very fond of John Gorman, as are most people in the game. He is widely recognised as being an excellent number two to the slightly more aloof Hoddle, and someone whom players at all levels like and trust. However, John questions whether John Gorman was the right appointment for the club or for Gorman personally.

'I know John had to think long and hard before accepting the job, and having discussed it with him years later I think he felt a little bit like I did when I was offered the managers job: if he hadn't taken it he would have felt he would never get the same opportunity again. Could John have kept us up? Yes is the answer. The quality of football the team played was still excellent. I lost count of the number of times that he came back from a match to say that we'd been told they were "the best footballing side they'd faced".

The problem was one of experience. John went for Andy Rowland as his assistant, who had never played or coached above the Third Division, and then in the summer, when I thought he needed to recruit a spine of the team, particularly in central-defence and up front, he signed players like Adrian Whitbread, Luc Nijholt and Jan Aage Fjortoft who had no top-flight experience. Now, the two lads, Nijholt and Fjortoft, were two of the best professionals I ever saw in terms of their attitude to the game, but they took a long time to settle in. Jan Aage didn't score until after Christmas, whilst I didn't think that Whitbread was good enough for that level.'

Towards the end of the season, Gorman did bring in some experience. A selection of older players, who, put bluntly, were well past their best, joined the club, people like Terry Fenwick, Frank McAvennie, and Lawrie Sanchez, but by then the damage was done. Swindon didn't win a game until the end of November, and although a good run between then and February gave them some hope, they were never off the bottom of the table and were comfortably relegated. They did score goals, but they conceded them at an alarming rate – seven at Newcastle, six at Everton and a number of fives, including 5–0 home defeats by both Liverpool and Leeds. The latter, on the last day of the season, took their League goals conceded tally to exactly 100, an unwanted Premiership record.

The difficulties on the pitch were put into perspective, though, by tragedy off the pitch, with the suicide of physiotherapist Kevin Morris during the season. Morris had been a long-term colleague of John, having fulfilled a variety of roles since joining the club in the 1960s, and his death affected not just John but everybody at the club.

'Kevin was in the reserves as a left-half under Bert Head, and although he never really made it as a player in the first team he served the club very well in a variety of roles, taking over as trainer when Harry Cousins left, and he was a great bloke. I'd worked with Kevin day in, day out for years, so, as you can imagine, his death was a huge shock.'

It is perhaps a good time at this point to pay tribute to a couple of other long-serving members of the backroom staff with whom John worked. They aren't household names, indeed probably their names will be known to only a few Swindon fans, but they both did great jobs for the club and were part of the reason why John enjoyed his time at the club so much. They helped the camaraderie that is part and parcel of any football club.

'I first got to know Eddie Buckley in the 1960s when he used to get the milk for us when we were training. Then he became the first aider round the club and my trainer with the youth team, before he became kit man under Glenn Hoddle. I think he's still at the club today, and clubs need people like him who do lots of work behind the scenes that the fans don't see.

There are some great stories about Eddie. His son, Sam, was a player under me in the youth team, and on one occasion Eddie was running the line in a game that Sam was playing in. Anyway, the ball went out of play on Eddie's side and he gave a thrown-in, much to the displeasure of Sam who had made the tackle. Sam started abusing Eddie so Eddie put his flag up, and the referee came over and reprimanded Sam. We gave Eddie some stick over that, I can tell you.

Eddie was also our trainer for the youth team. Once he came running on the pitch to treat a player and caused chaos. In those days he had a bladder with a sponge in it to administer to the injured player. On this occasion he put the bladder down, finished treating the player and then ran off with the match ball instead of the bladder!

The best story about Eddie, though, concerns a game at Spurs with the reserves. One of our players got injured, and Eddie came running on, only to stop in the centre circle – his back had gone. So on came the St John Ambulance team and carried off our trainer with his medical bag! It was actually quite bad, so we arranged for him to go to Princes Margaret Hospital in Swindon when we got back. The hospital staff were waiting there with an emergency trolley ready to admit him. When we got to reception they wanted some details, and when I told them that he was 54 and the trainer/physio they fell about laughing because Kevin Morris had called them and told them that an injured player from Swindon Town would be coming in, and they weren't expecting Eddie. They found it hilarious, as we all did, that it was our own medical man who was injured!

The other person who I spent years working with at the club was Terry Wollen. Terry and I go back a long way. You will remember that we made our first-team debuts on the same day, and when I went into youth-team coaching he worked with me there until I left the club. He was really good with kids and a good coach. Again, few Swindon supporters will have seen the work he did behind the scenes, but, like Eddie and Kevin, he worked really hard for the club.'

Back in the First Division for the 1994–95 season, hopes were high of a quick return, but the start was poor and, with the club's finances now geared to Premiership not First Division football, the board decided they had to act. In November 1994 Gorman was sacked and the board decided to go back to their previously successful policy of appointing a young, untried player-manager. The man they selected was Steve McMahon. It was the beginning of the end of John's time at Swindon.

A young John Trollope in training, early on in his career.

Wedding day – John and Maureen pictured with members of the Swindon Town team in 1965.

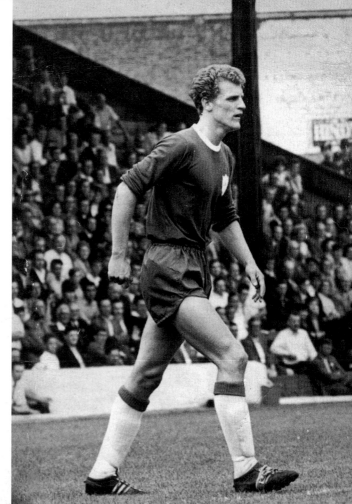

John in League action in the 1960s.

John in action during Swindon's match at West Ham in January 1967.

John lines up for the annual, pre-season photo shoot in 1967. He is second from the left on the back row, next to his great friend Don Rogers.

A portrait picture of John taken during Swindon's 1968-69 season.

The side that John still feels is the best he ever played in – The Swindon
Town side of 1969–70. John is fourth from the right on the back row.

It wasn't just football. John (middle, front row) lines up with a selection of
Swindon Town players for a game of cricket.

John receives the first of many awards – this one was to mark his 250th League appearance at the club.

John coaches a young Paul in the back garden of his home at Highworth.

John in typical action
during the mid-1970s in a
game against Luton.

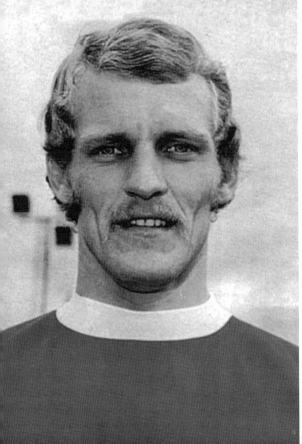

A profile of John taken
from *Shoot* magazine in
1974.

"JOHN – THE TRUE PROFESSIONAL" –
AND STILL ONLY 31 !*
(AND SO LOYAL)

THE TIME LESS ROBIN

THE GALLANT 600
AND ALL THE CUP & OTHER ONES!

ALL GOOD WISHES from BILL PAU...
15 Feb. 197...

A cartoon drawn for John to celebrate his 600th League appearance for Swindon.

John and Paul in Swindon Town kit, taken on Paul's third birthday in 1975.

Older pro John in action during one of his many come-backs, away at Hull City.

Youth-team boss John lines up with the Swindon Town squad ahead of the 1978–79 season.

"Eighteen years with Swindon . . . and you end up turning out for The Palace!"
Submitted by reader Dave Hollister, of Wootton Bassett.

A cartoon published in the local Swindon paper, the *Evening Advertiser*, to mark John's MBE in 1978.

John in action during the game where he broke the record for the most League appearances for one club against Carlisle in October 1980. The Carlisle player in the picture is Peter Beardsley, who later went on to be a successful England International.

Manager John Trollope
in his office shortly
after becoming boss.

John's daughter, Sara.

The manager meets
some young fans.

Back to youth-team boss. John pictured after returning to the youth-team job.

THIRTY-SEVEN
YEARS... AND OUT

Steve McMahon arrived at Swindon with a reputation for being one of football's hard men. In a career that had seen him play at the top flight for Everton, Aston Villa, and Liverpool, as well as England, he had tenaciously patrolled the midfield, getting embroiled in more than his fair share of on-the-pitch arguments. What was not in doubt was his drive and desire to win.

He made an immediate impact. After seeing his new charges lose 2–1 at home to Luton on 26 November 1994, he complained that there hadn't been enough commitment from his team, citing as evidence the fact that nobody had been booked from his side. The following week McMahon made his playing debut at Southend. He promptly showed that he intended to practice what he preached – he was sent off.

On the pitch in the League, McMahon's arrival made little difference as the club continued to struggle at the wrong end of the table. Some compensation was another epic run in the League Cup, which brought a third semi-final in John's time at Swindon, this time against Bolton. As in 1980 against Wolves, Swindon won the first leg 2–1 but lost the second leg 3–1 to see the end of their Wembley dreams. Division One survival now became the sole focus.

Off the pitch, John was finding his new boss difficult. Still youth-team manager, the easy relationships he had enjoyed with all his previous bosses, from Bobby Smith through to John Gorman, were now a thing of the past.

'Steve McMahon very rarely talked to me and didn't get involved with the youth side of the game at all. He never came to the centre of excellence and hardly ever came to watch the youth team. He seemed not to want to know, and could be very rude and abrupt when he wanted to be, not just to me but to others on the staff as well. Nothing was said to me directly, though, so I carried on doing my job as I'd always done.'

Despite the goals of new signing Peter Thorne from Blackburn Rovers, Swindon were unable to preserve their First Division status. The glory of the Play-off Final win two years previously was now a distant memory as they slid to a second successive relegation.

The following season, 1995–96, saw Swindon playing outside the top two Leagues of English football for the first time since 1986–87. McMahon brought in new players and the side responded, with a good start seeing them hitting the top of the League early on. They never looked like missing out on promotion, and for the second time in the club's League history went on to finish top of the table, claiming the Second Division Championship in mid-April. By then, John had left the club.

John is convinced that, ironically, Swindon's success on the pitch was a key factor in him losing his job. With the first team winning, McMahon's position in the club was hugely strengthened, and he was able to demand changes, knowing that his power would mean he would get his way. The writing for John was on the wall early on in the season.

'Tommy Wheeldon, who had been with McMahon at Everton, was brought in to replace Adrian Riddiford, who had been running youth development with me. Initially, Wheeldon asked if he could observe me on the training pitch, which I had no problem with. It was only after I left that I realised he was getting himself ready to take over my job. Another Liverpudlian, Phil Cannons, was brought in as youth development officer as McMahon lined himself up with a load of mates on the staff.

I was definitely on the outside. A lot of the staff used to go off and play golf during the week, and I was criticised for not going, but it was impractical with all the work I had to do with my youth job.

The youth-team coach at any club is often first in and last out. People in the club were saying that I should watch my back, but I didn't see it coming.'

'It' was the sack. On Friday 18 March McMahon called John into the manager's office and told him that he wanted him out of the club. There had been signs that all was not well, but it was still a huge shock.

'I will never forget what happened. It was one of the worst days of my life. I had been preparing the youth team as usual on a Friday for Saturday's match, which that weekend was at Brighton – strange how details like that can stick isn't it? Anyway, I was told to go and see the manager, and out of the blue he told me he wanted me to leave immediately. As anybody would do in that situation, I asked why and he told me he wasn't happy with what I was doing on the training ground and that there hadn't been enough players coming through from the youth team into the first team. He also told me, which I thought was a bit rich coming from him, that some of the players didn't like me. I would dispute that. Sure the odd one or two would be unhappy, but the vast majority of players who have worked under me would say that although I was strict, I was fair and consistent.'

John, as anybody who knows him will tell you, is a loyal and private man. Until this book he has refused all offers to give his side of the story. Indeed, he still believes that even if he had agreed to give his view when he was sacked, the club would have stopped any views of his being written or broadcast. This is the first time he has spoken of his views as to what happened.

'McMahon just wanted me out because, for some reason, my face didn't fit. How he could make a judgement on my coaching ability when he never saw me coach is beyond me. Clearly it wasn't based on his direct experience, but somebody was giving him ammunition behind my back. And as for the players coming through, I could point to a number who had come through in recent seasons, and in the team he had Wayne O'Sullivan who had come through the ranks, and he had only recently sold Andy Thomson to Portsmouth.

The thing that still sticks in my throat is that there was no warning. I think anybody should know if they need to change and to be given a chance to make those changes. If they cannot do it then, fair enough, take action. At no stage had anything been said to me that people were unhappy with what I was doing on the training pitch. Sure, I knew I didn't fit in with McMahon and his mates, but surely that's not enough reason to get rid of somebody.'

John had previously been promised a 'job for life' by various directors at the club, both past and present. Now, after 37 years' continuous service, that promise was blown away. Nobody on the board, at least to John's knowledge, stuck up for him. He wrote a letter to Mike Spearman, the then Chairman, complaining about his treatment. All he got back was a polite letter saying that the board felt that they had to back the manager. There was no note of thanks for his service over the years. Sadly, John has become estranged from the club that was his life for so long.

'I've never had a note of thanks from the club for what I did. I don't think that would have taken much to do really, given how few people spend as long as I did at the club. I've only ever been invited back to the club once by a club official, that was Mike Sullivan, the marketing manager. The board of directors have never invited me back to anything. It even upsets me, which perhaps it shouldn't, that in the redeveloped club, that whilst quite rightly there are suites named after people who have done a lot for Swindon, like Don Rogers and Danny Williams, there are suites named after others who have done less, and there is nothing named after Maurice Owen and I who are the two longest-serving Swindon players ever.

I just don't think that the club looks after its old players in the way some teams do. Travelling the country like I do, you hear lots of people say that they are going to this event and that event for former players, organised by their old club. Swindon do nothing, which I think is very sad indeed.

It took me a long time to get over the way I was treated. For a long time I refused to have anything red at all, if I got a company car, I would say "I hope it isn't red!" Over time, I've mellowed a bit, and as Swindon are one of the clubs that I've dealt with in my Football League role I do go back there from time to time and deal with the situation. When Paul finishes playing I've said to Maureen that I will go back and watch them on a regular basis. You don't lose affection for a club that's been such a big part of your life so easily. But I do wish it all ended differently, and that the club had handled things since in a better way.'

It is a sobering story and a sad reflection on the way football is run. Thirty-seven years' service and dismissed without warning. Small wonder that people in the game are accused of being 'out for themselves'. One is left asking, what is the price for loyalty?

It is important to understand John's biggest disappointment with the way things were handled. It wasn't so much that he lost his job as youth-team coach but the fact that there was no warning. He's been in the game long enough to know that any job in football – playing, managing or coaching – is precarious, however, he hoped that he would have been warned, given his years of service to the club, that his position was under threat. More than that, he might reasonably have expected that the club (who, after all, employ the manager, not the other way round) could have found an alternative role for him when McMahon decided he wanted to make a change, particularly given the promises of 'a job for life'. The fact that this didn't happen is what upset him then and still does to this day.

Rather than end this chapter on a downbeat note, lets end it on a humorous note instead. John tells the story of a trip back to the County Ground in his monitor role. While there, he had a meeting with some members of Swindon's staff about a query he had on his pension contributions made while he was a player. Someone senior in the club, who shall remain nameless, was in the meeting and uttered the memorable lines 'I didn't know you'd played, John. Who did you play for?'

LIFE AFTER SWINDON

Thirty-seven years is a long time to spend with one employer, so it is not surprising that John took time to adjust after leaving Swindon. With hindsight, he can see that although the circumstances surrounding his departure from the club were painful and less than ideal the break from football did him good.

'Clearly it was difficult at first, not just getting used to not having a job to go into but also coming to terms with the way that I felt I'd been treated by the club. However, looking back I think the time I had away from full-time football did me good – it meant that when I went back into the game I felt I was fresher and had recharged my batteries. At the time, I probably hadn't appreciated how much the last 18 months at Swindon had taken out of me.'

John kept his hand in over the next few months by helping his old friend Don Rogers run soccer schools in Swindon and Melksham, and it was over the summer of 1996 that he found the job he would do for the next 10 months – that of postman. It is perhaps not surprising that a number of former footballers (former England and Nottingham Forest midfielder Neil Webb being perhaps the most high-profile example) end up as posties. It has a number of attractions for those who have been in the game, not least the fact that it keeps them outdoors and physically fit. For John it was an excellent job.

'I was taking an FA Preliminary Coaching Badge course for the Wiltshire FA in the summer of 1996, and on that course was a postman from Marlborough. Anyway, we got chatting and the more he talked about what he did the more it appealed, so I decided to apply and was fortunate enough to be taken on.

I loved it. Sure you had to get up early in the morning, but that had never been a problem so it didn't worry me, getting up to be in the office at 5.30. Then you had the morning, from 7.00am, delivering post, after which your day was your own. I found the job very relaxing and stress-free, which was a complete change from how I felt in my latter days in football. It was good being out and about, and I very much enjoyed my round, which was in Chiseldon.'

In the summer of 1997, after John had been a postman for 10 months, the opportunity presented itself to move back into full-time football. The club that came calling was one of Swindon's local rivals, Bristol Rovers, whose then manager, Ian Holloway, approached John to run the club's centre of excellence – testimony to the regard in which John was held within the game for his work with youngsters.

'I did have to think about it for a while because I had enjoyed my time out of football, but in the end the lure of going back into the game proved too strong. I'd only been there a short time when the club's youth-team coach, Geoff Twentyman, resigned to move full time into the media, and as a result of this I was asked to run the youth team as well.

I very much enjoyed it at the start. I had the youngsters playing the way that Glenn Hoddle had shown me at Swindon – in a 3–5–2 formation with a sweeper – and they responded really well to it. We had some good results, and I thought that the quality of some of the football that we played, with the movement and passing, was very good.'

It all started to go wrong, though, in the autumn when Ian Holloway called together all the coaches at the club and told them he wanted all the teams to play in the same way as the first team, which at that time was a rigid 4–4–2 formation.

'I was very surprised. We had been playing well and getting some decent results, and I must admit it was the beginning of the end for me at the club when he said that. What made it worse was that he then decided the best way to explain was to come and demonstrate to the youngsters what he wanted to do, so he turned up at one of our training sessions with a piece of rope. What he did was to get the back four to hold the piece of rope together and to move up and down the pitch with that rope. His instructions to them were that "they should never break the rope joining them together". This, of course, meant that, whilst they now defended as a unit, there was no scope for the full-backs to go forward because they were being told to be level with the central defenders. Not my type of game at all.'

Initially, John followed instructions, while inwardly, no doubt, seething at what he saw as an attempt to restrain creativity and thinking on the pitch. However, matters came to a head after a game at Brighton.

'Brighton seem to have played an important part in my latter career don't they?! Anyway we played down there in a youth-team match, and at the start we played in the way that I'd been told to tell them to, but it wasn't going well and with 20 minutes or so to go we were losing. In desperation, I switched back to the way that I preferred – the 3–5–2 formation. We improved markedly and we won the game. On the Monday I was called into Holloway's office and asked why I hadn't had the team playing in the way I'd been told to do – someone had obviously snitched on me.

I stuck it out for a bit longer, but then I went into the manager's office and asked if it would change, because I wasn't enjoying the way we were playing, and when I was told "no" I resigned on principle. I don't blame Ian Holloway – he was just trying to do what he thought was best for the club, and he had a group of first-team players who he felt were best suited to playing a rigid 4–4–2, so that's what he did. However, for me there was no development for the younger players in playing the way that the first team did. They weren't getting basic grounding in passing and movement, and I think that is critical for players at that age, so that they are able to play in a variety of systems later on in their career. Yes, it was another big decision to resign, but as I wasn't enjoying it I felt it was the right thing to do.'

John resigned in March 1998 and returned to his previous job as a postman. This time it was a short-lived stint delivering the mail because in

the summer of 1998 he was back in football, working for the Football League as a regional monitor for youth development. No, I didn't know what one of these was either!

'Back in 1998 the first youth academies were being set up, and the clubs were getting grant-aided funding from a combination of Sport England and the Premier League. My job was to make sure they were complying with what they said they would do with the money when they prepared a development document – a sort of business plan – to get the money. I had the role of looking after 17 clubs, making six official visits per season to see how things were going, dealing mainly with the centre of excellence managers and the academy managers. It was a big patch as well – 17 clubs in all, from Plymouth to Swansea, Bournemouth to Notts County, and Leicester to Shrewsbury. I very much enjoyed it to start with, but over the last two years I've found it a bit more repetitive with too much administration. The job has got more difficult in some ways as well since the collapse of the ITV Digital TV deal, which has left a number of clubs with financial problems, and, therefore, cutting back on their youth programmes.'

John, as by now you will have observed, is not one to do a job if he's not enjoying it, so it will come as no surprise to learn that as this book was being written his career in football took a new, and possibly final, turn when he resigned from his regional monitor job.

'I just felt that I wanted to get back into working at a club again for what I think will be my final job before I retire at 65. I had an offer from Chelsea to do some scouting, but I see myself as a coach rather than as a scout, which is something I've never really done much of, so I turned it down to go back into coaching. In the end I have decided to do a couple of jobs. One is assessing for the Premier League at the Saturday morning youth games – quality of the pitches, the facilities and the hospitality, that sort of thing. The other is to do some coaching at Wolves, which has been one of the clubs in my Football League job and where I've got to know the academy staff very well. I'm really looking forward to this, although

I shall take quite a significant drop in earnings because the Wolves job will only be a couple of evenings a week, together with the Sunday morning matches. Coaching kids is what gives me the biggest pleasure, and it's great to get back on the training ground.

John has, over the years, developed a very good reputation as a coach. Those who have worked with him are universally complimentary about his ability with youngsters, both on and off the pitch. He is rightly proud of the number of players he has brought through to first-team football, other than Paul Rideout, perhaps not household names but good, solid professionals – people like Charlie Henry, Brian Hughes, Colin Baillie, Paul Batty and Rideout himself in the early 1980s, through to Mark Gardiner, Fitzroy Simpson, Adie Viveash, Paul Hunt and Nicky Summerbee in the late 1980s and early 1990s, and then Andy Thompson, Wayne O'Sullivan, Steve Mildenhall and Sol Davis towards the end of his time at Swindon

'I've enjoyed every minute coaching youngsters, working with them and seeing them develop, some to professional standard, others to a good non-League standard. I felt that most players responded to my methods, although of course one or two would always rebel. I always encouraged them to play football, teaching them that football is simple game and that movement off the ball and personal fitness was key. I emphasised the importance of being dedicated and professional on and off the pitch. Most of the lads I see now appreciate what I did and that the work they did with me stood them in good stead, regardless of what level they played at.'

So, by the time you read this, John will be back doing what he loves most, coaching and developing youngsters. And, given that the manager of Wolves, as the book is written, is his old friend Glenn Hoddle, it's a fair bet that he won't be asked to do things he doesn't believe in!

TRAINING

Nowadays, the way in which managers and, more particularly, the 'coaches' prepare their players for matches is finely tuned. Nothing is left to chance. There are fitness coaches, sports psychologists and specialist coaches for each position on the pitch. Diet and nutrition is carefully monitored and every move is captured by video cameras.

Back in the 1960s things were very different, and, although John saw some changes during his long playing, managerial and coaching career, it is only in recent years that some of the major changes have occurred.

The first difference is in the name. Now we have a preponderance of coaches. Back then there was one person doing the lot, known to all and sundry as the trainer. The first man to make an impression on John, besides the schoolteachers and Swindon Boys teachers already recorded, was the assistant manager to Bert Head, Ellis Stuttard.

'One of the best sessions I ever did for my development was without a ball. I remember Ellis Stuttard, the old trainer, taking me out on the County Ground pitch, probably in my first season as a professional. What he did was move himself round the pitch and ask me where I should be positioning myself, firstly without the ball then with the ball, and then with other players as opponents. That's how I got my positional sense, from those sessions. I used to kick a few off the line in the early days and it was all down to Ellis and his training, someone taking time to teach me the tools of the game.'

The training sessions John participated in as a young professional were, to his mind, much more focused on developing the basics than similar sessions would be today.

'In some ways, modern professionals would recognise a lot of what we were doing. We did a lot of things you will see on the training ground today – ball work in twos, practising controlling the ball on your thigh and chest, learning how to the kick the ball properly and the like. The differences, though, were in the emphasis. We spent a lot of time learning the basics of football – how to kick the ball properly, how to control the ball on the first touch, how to play in the position that you were playing in. I'm not sure as much time is spent on this today.

The other difference was the fitness training. Nowadays a lot of time is spent working on what they call 'football-related runs'. We worked much more on stamina, doing long runs of maybe three, four or five miles. We used to call it endurance back then. I've personally never minded running, and I know those long runs helped me. Playing as an overlapping full-back, I used to regularly run 60 to 70 yards up the wing to support Don Rogers and then run back again almost as quickly as I'd run up the pitch. The other thing to remember is that pitches were much worse back then, you needed to have stamina because there was mud everywhere. I hear some of today's players complain about the pitch when there are a few divots around. The pitches are like billiard tables compared to what we used to play on.'

John is still very much involved in the game and having working for the Football League he is well placed to see what currently happens with today's youngsters.

'Some of what they call what they do makes me laugh. There is a lot of emphasis at the moment on "lateral movement" – SAQ is what they call it. We used to do exercises to improve our "lateral movement", but they were much simpler than what they do today. We used to zig-zag between the edge of the pitch and the advertising hoardings. We didn't have gyms with the latest fitness equipment to build up our strength; we used to run at the old training ground at Shrivenham Road carrying railway sleepers.' [Appropriately enough for an old railway town, one thinks. I wonder if other teams also ran carrying symbols of what had made the town famous?!]

I asked John what he thinks is the single biggest difference today. The response was instant.

'I think we were given much more freedom to express ourselves than players do today, both on the pitch and on the training ground. The training today is much more structured, and players are expected to play to a certain game plan, which often is based on the manager's fear of losing. Now, I'm not saying that is all down to the managers because they are given so little time to get results today, but some of it is, and it doesn't just apply to the first team. I've seen matches at under-13 level where coaches have told players to "hold back". Surely, at that age, if they want to express themselves by going forward then they should be allowed to.

In all my career I was given very few instructions on how to play the game. I was just told to go out and play football. The only manager who tried to change my game was Fred Ford. He used to complain at me overlapping all the time, so I used to apologise to him and then do exactly the same the next game. It was part of the way I played football. Harry Cousins, the old player who became trainer, was the only other player to give me specific advice, and those people who knew Harry would not be surprised to know that the advice was to "hit my winger in the first five minutes, on the halfway line, to let him know I was around!"'

How about tactics? Today's teams spend a lot of time working on ever more intricate set-pieces, hoping against hope that they can execute properly when a similar situation arises in a game. It was a bit less planned in John's day

'We did very little work on set-pieces. Back then the standard corner was the away-swinger, so, although Don or whoever was taking the corner might practise striking the ball right, we didn't have elaborate routines like they do today.'

Diet and nutrition are two areas where there have been significant changes over the last few years, influenced, in no small way, by the influx of overseas players and managers. Forty years ago life was very different.

'I ate what I liked. Nobody ever told me that I couldn't or

shouldn't. It would make people laugh now. We used to have steak at lunchtime on the morning of a match [I am temporarily transported back to the early 1970s and my prized collection of *Shoot* magazines, with their weekly feature asking a top player banal questions like favourite food? Everybody put down steak, with or without chips. John is quick to deny that he ever had chips with his steak pre-match, although he does admit to regularly following the steak with rice pudding!]. Nowadays, with red meat being one of the foods which takes longest to digest, that would be one of the worst things!'

Not only was the pre-match meal different, so was the pre-match and post-match preparation.

'We never did any warm-ups before the game at all. I used to run out for the first time on a Saturday afternoon at five to three. I do wonder at some of the warm-ups you see today. Are they being done for the benefit of the players or so the crowd can see that the coach can put on a good session? Equally, things like cool-downs after the game, together with ice-baths, were a long way off. I always used to like a long, hot soak in the bath, which would now be viewed as the worst thing you can do.

We were never encouraged to rehydrate after and during games. I did have a glass of water at half-time, but only because I don't like tea, which is what the other players drank. After the game players would go to the supporters' club bar and have a couple of pints. There were no players' bars back then, and relationships between players and supporters were much closer than they are today. At Swindon we had a brilliant supporters' club, and as it was very much a community club; most of the players knew the regular supporters very well.'

John is not against some of the changes and innovations that have come into the game, but he does feel that there is too much 'rubbishing' of the old days.

'I went on my UEFA 'A' conversion course to convert from the old course to the new one a couple of years back and did the fitness module. I sat through the whole morning listening to what you should do now, and thought we didn't do any of this. Anyway, at the end of the morning I said to the guy running the course "I used to play and we didn't do this, but we were still fit and played more games than most people do now, so we must have done something right." I don't think he knew that I'd played for 20 seasons and barely missed any games!'

Talking of injuries leads us to talk of how they were treated. John, of course, can count his injuries on the fingers of one hand: a stomach muscle strain, a groin strain, a hamstring (caused by making a cross to create a goal for Don Rogers against Liverpool, but more of that later) and a broken arm. Not bad for a 20-year career! John, however, still had some stories to tell of how injuries were dealt with in the 1960s via the Swindon trainer Harry Cousins.

'Harry was trainer and psychologist all rolled into one. He would never have called it psychology, it was more like kidology really. His two big targets were Don Rogers and Frank Burrows. With Don it was always "just heard who's coming to watch you on Saturday Don. They'll all want to see you turn in a show, these scouts." Frank was always on the treatment table so Harry was always saying "Frank we really need you playing on Saturday – they can't manage without you, you know."

He was brilliant. You couldn't have wished for a better person to have as trainer. Mind you we used to moan at him. As Don said in his book, you would take your boots to him for a new pair because the right boot had fallen apart, and he would look at you and say "what's wrong with the left one?"

He used to trick players as well. He often treated injuries by using an old heating lamp. He'd direct the lamp on the injury, go off for 10 minutes, come back and feel the injury and say "much better, that's done the trick". Then you'd discover that he hadn't even switched the lamp on! When Kevin Morris took over as trainer he found an old notebook of Harry's where all the injuries were documented over several season. Harry had one line which said what the injury was, and then another one that said what the course of treatment was. In many cases, after the injury saying groin strain or sore knee or whatever, he had written "fannying" or "malingering!" But we all loved him to bits.'

So, finally, how does John compare the training regimes of the different managers he played under or coached with? His response makes fascinating reading.

'With Bert Head it was as you would expect, pretty basic but hard work and very, very disciplined – you didn't mess around with Bert. I would say the sessions were quite regimented, although we did spend a lot of time focusing on doing the basics right with a ball. With Danny Williams it was much more laid back, and off-the-cuff we had one hard running day, always a Thursday, but provided we did that properly Danny was very relaxed.

Fred Ford was the best coach I worked with in many ways. He was very well organised, and because he had been a coach before becoming a manager, and was what they used to call a staff coach, he'd done his coaching course, which was very unusual at the time, he was quite prepared to try new things. After Fred came Dave Mackay. All we used to do with him was five-a-sides, which I think was mainly for his benefit to be honest.

Les Allen used to have a trainer working with him called Gordon Eddlestone who'd come from Wolves. To be honest he used to think he was Bill McGarry [the former Wolves manager] and didn't treat us with much respect, which got the players annoyed. He used to belittle us by doing things like making us wait for training. After Danny's second spell we had Bob Smith with Wilf Tranter as his assistant, and you can start to see some modern thinking creeping in. When I came back from retirement under Bob in 1980 I did warm-ups before the game, the first time I'd ever done that in 20 years as a professional.'

Looking through my notes, I see that we didn't talk about the reign of Ken Beamish, who had a brief spell as manager in the mid-1980s, not a happy time for the club as we have seen, so perhaps best forgotten.

Moving on to more modern times, and Swindon's famous trio of player-managers…

'Lou Macari placed enormous importance on players being fit and hard-working, so we used to do running most days – short runs, long runs, you name it, we used to do it. Then we had Ossie Ardiles, and the contrast was huge. All the work was done with a ball, and he trusted each player to keep themselves fit. Ossie really didn't like running at all. I remember that I took the youth team out on a run around the lanes in the summer, and he saw me and told me off for going too fast! Ossie's pre-seasons were the easiest I've ever seen in all my years in the game, and I think in his second season he suffered for it. The first season all the players were fit from playing under Lou, but over a period of time, with no real emphasis on fitness and a very light pre-season, their physical condition suffered, and that affected the performances on the pitch.

Finally, there was Glenn Hoddle, who had just come from a spell in France, where, of course, he'd worked with Arsene Wenger. This was much more modern training. I remember he was doing one exercise with the players, and he was telling them when and how to breathe, it was "inhale now" and "exhale now". I'd never seen anything like it. However, he was very good in his training sessions, lots of new ideas, and I think he was better balanced than Lou or Ossie in terms of getting players to do ball work and concentrate on their physical fitness.'

So, clearly times have changed. John can see that some of the training changes would have helped him. As a naturally fit player and athlete, though, perhaps they would have helped him less than many others of his generation.

LIFE AS A PROFESSIONAL

Times have changed since John played professional football. Although his last first-team game was nearly 25 years ago he has remained in the game since then, and is still involved today. He is, therefore, well placed to observe the differences between then and now.

One of the key differences is not so much about football but about life today. In some ways, travelling across England today is easier than it has ever been. While there are more cars than ever on the roads, most of the country is served by a fast (usually!) motorway network. Indeed, for longer trips the increase in availability of air travel means that there is now another mode of transport. Back in the 1960s things were very different.

'Travelling was much harder back then, I'm sure of it, and it was the one thing that I didn't enjoy as a professional footballer. Not only were the journeys long, but I'm not a great coach traveller anyway.

We were travelling before the motorways, which meant that every trip north was a major expedition. For example, it used to take us five hours to get to Sheffield – up through towns like Leicester and Ashby-de-la-Zouch – and when I say through, I mean through the town centres, it took ages. The coaches were a bit different as well, not the air-conditioned luxury coaches you get now with videos and microwaves on board, these were good, old-fashioned coaches, which rattled along. I don't think they could go above 40 or 50 miles an hour.

Some of the journeys were absolutely horrendous. I remember

going to Hull for a game and getting stuck in the snow, and all the players had to get off and try and dig the coach out in freezing conditions, which was no fun, particularly when the coach was almost as cold inside as it was outside! We had one trip to Grimsby for a night game when we left Swindon on the morning of the game, probably about 9.30 in the morning, and got back at half past five in the morning.

On that trip I will always remember Freddie Jones, a young winger who played a few games for us in the sixties, trying to sleep on the parcel shelf. He was very small, and he just climbed up there and curled up! Most of the time, for long away fixtures on a Saturday we travelled up the day before, much as you'd do now. We tended to stay in the same places, one hotel near Sheffield for the trips to Yorkshire and the North-East and one hotel just south of Manchester for trips to the North-West. We had a few scrapes on those trips I can tell you, but nothing we can put in this book – what goes on tour, stays on tour!

The journeys were very boring – I did join in the card school occasionally, but most of the time I sat at the front, because I wasn't a great traveller, and talked to the driver. It wasn't fun, but you just had to get on with it.'

How about the places John visited? As you would expect from somebody who had such a long playing career, he played on most League grounds (John can only recall five teams that he never played 'away' against, including, sadly for him, Manchester United). He also played at the home grounds of a number of teams who are no longer in the League, including Workington, Barrow, Bradford Park Avenue, Southport and Newport County.

'Some of the grounds we went to were appalling really. No disrespect to them, but Hartlepool's ground was pretty basic, and as for Barrow, the bath was through a hole in the dressing room wall – you had to step through the hole before you could have a soak! Fellows Park, Walsall's old ground, was very cramped as well. I remember we played once there and were losing by three or four goals when the fog came down and the game was abandoned – we had to rescue Mike Summerbee who was out there somewhere!

It was different back then, because clubs didn't get money to develop their grounds like you do today – there were no grants from the Football Trust. As a result grounds tended to be unchanged, year in year out, and slowly got more and more decrepit. It's only recently that grounds have been rebuilt or, in some cases, teams have moved grounds completely.'

How about the better grounds, after all John played at over 100 League grounds during his playing career, including some of the most well-known grounds in the country

'My favourite grounds were in the North-East, Sunderland, at the old Roker Park, and Newcastle. We tended to get well beaten there, but the atmosphere was great. You were just in awe at the size of the crowds and how big the grounds were, banks of terracing filled with passionate fans.

I did play at Highbury as well, which would be one of the best grounds, obviously, but I'm not sure whether it counts as it was a reserve-team fixture. I was managing and playing sweeper for the reserves. I must have been over 40, and we came up against a young player called Raphael Meade; he could give me a 10 yard start in a race over 15 yards and still beat me. We lost heavily, and I think I realised then I should probably call it a day completely!'

We move on to talking about the profile of being a footballer. John has lived all his life near the town in which he made his name, and has lived in Highworth, just outside Swindon, since 1973. He was, as both a player and a manager, very recognisable in the town. How did he cope with the attention?

'It's different now from how it used to be, in that I don't think the relationships between the players and the press and media are anywhere near as good as they once were. Obviously, I can only comment at a local level because I've never been a high-profile player like a Don Rogers, Ernie Hunt or Mike Summerbee, but, even so, I think things have changed. Back then the media used to let you get on with your life. You would have a chat with them but what you did off the pitch was your own business, and you didn't get the press reporting you for having a drink in the town. Often, they might be drinking in the same pubs or going to the same restaurants as we did.

You didn't have the same media coverage, of course, which helped. Now every game is on television; then, if you were a club like Swindon, you might be covered once or twice a season. With that coverage comes much more pressure – all the different camera angles and then all the TV programmes to fill with comments and phone-ins to stir things up.

Relationships with the fans were different as well. Swindon was always a community club where a lot of the supporters knew the players and vice versa. We never used to mind chatting to them. In fact, the old Swindon Town Supporters' Club were a great bunch and did a lot for the club. Of course, you'd get recognised. Maureen and I used to go out for meals in Swindon with Don and Jane Rogers, and people used to always come up and say hello, but generally your privacy was respected and people were very friendly.

I was very fortunate in that I got on very well with the fans. I was a trier, and I think fans generally like players who clearly give their all for a club. The only stick I used to get was from one bloke who stood in the old Shrivenham Road stand, at the Stratton Bank end. Every game I used to hear him saying things like "you're useless Trollope" or "you still here Trollope?" and generally giving me a hard time. In the end it just became a bit of a joke!'

Overall, John considers himself to be a lucky person

'I was very fortunate on two counts. Firstly, I played football for a living, which was a great job, and one that most people never have the chance of doing. Secondly, I played in what I believe was a great era for football – the 1960s, a time where the game was played in the right spirit and the pressures were a lot less than they are today. There was so much I enjoyed about the job, from the training, which because I enjoyed keeping fit wasn't really a chore, through to the camaraderie of playing with some great people who I got on with, which was definitely the case in the 1960s. I can't see how I couldn't have enjoyed it.'

Today many professionals live a fairly pampered existence, with most of their needs met by the club, but it wasn't always the case...

'We always looked after our own kit. When I was living at home my mum used to wash the training kit, and then Maureen took over that job when we got married. My dad used to clean my boots for me when I was a young professional, and he used to scrub and boil the white laces, which went in the boots. I would then blacken them before the game – dad never knew.'

Perhaps the biggest changes in football since John played is in the area of financial reward. Even at the top level very, very few players from his era made enough money from their time as players to live comfortably at the end of their career, and John, as a player who played exclusively at the second and third levels of English football, is no exception, which is no surprise when you consider the level of earnings he enjoyed during his career.

'I started on £5 as a member of the groundstaff in 1959, and then this was increased to £10 a week when I signed professional terms in the summer of 1960, although the wage dropped to £7 in the summer. I also got a win bonus, which for years and years was £4 a win, home or away, and £2 for a draw, together with a small bonus for each first-team game I played in.

Wages just didn't go up very quickly in the first part of my career. I was only on £30 a week basic wage the year we won the League Cup, and the most I ever earned as a professional was around £150 a week, which was right at the end of my career.'

Ah, yes, the League Cup – surely that was a good payday for the players.

'Obviously I can only talk for myself, but I got the same win bonus, £4, as I was getting for any other game that we won. There was nothing in our contracts about getting a bonus for winning the Cup because nobody thought it was relevant. The only thing that we did benefit from was the fact that in our contracts it said that we would get £1 for each 1,000 on the gate above 12,000, so with the gate at Wembley being 100,000 we all got an extra £88 that week. The club also gave us a watch as a memento, but it wasn't a huge financial windfall for any of us, although we weren't that bothered at the time really.'

Once his playing career finished, again John didn't reap huge financial rewards.

'When I became manager I know, because I saw all of the contracts, that a number of players were on as much, if not a bit more, than me. I think to some degree I was hampered by the fact that I was already on the staff so the club didn't feel they needed to pay me as much as an outsider. In my youth roles, I've always been fairly paid, but it isn't the most lucrative job at a football club so you don't make a huge amount of money there, not that it bothers me hugely because it is the job I wanted to do. Sometimes when people know that I've been in football I think they assume that I've made a lot of money, but I can tell you that isn't the case.'

So, given this, how does John feel about the financial rewards available to today's players?

'The thing I struggle with is not just the amount of money available, I mean £100,000 a week is just ridiculous, isn't it? But the fact that you've got such big differentials in the way players in the same team are paid. Football is a team game, and, whilst I accept that certain players will always command more money than others, I think it's very wrong that some players on the same team will be paid say £60,000 a week while others are on £10,000 a week. I don't think that can help team spirit, and it doesn't reflect what happens on the pitch, one player doesn't win a match by himself no matter how good he is.

If you look back to the team I played in I am sure that someone like Don would have been on more money than me, which I have no problems with at all, but I am sure he wouldn't have been on six times more than me!'

So who does John blame for this explosion in wages?

'I'm afraid some of it has to lie at the hands of the boards of directors. Most people who run football clubs have come into the game after a good career in business, and you have to ask whether they would run their businesses the way they run their football clubs.

It should be very obvious that, long term, you cannot have more money going out than you have coming in, yet some clubs seem to carry on spending on players wages without seeming to think about the long-term consequences of what they are doing. I know that Boards will say that if they don't pay a player what he wants then that player will go elsewhere, but someone, somewhere, needs to make a stand and not pay silly wages and be prepared to stand up to the players and their agents. The people who end up suffering are the fans. The players move on, often the directors do too, and the people left to rebuild the club are the fans, who don't move on they loyally follow their club through thick and thin.

It's important to realise that there is no bitterness in what John says. He has enjoyed his career in football, and he has a good standard of living. Besides, money has never been that important to him, his focus has always been more on his family and their happiness.

We talk about what can be done to help put football back on a sound financial footing. John has some clear ideas in this regard.

'I think that we should go back to the old days of paying players only when they are playing – make contracts more linked to performance if you like. For example, I don't see why we shouldn't go back to the old days when you used to get less in the summer than you did during the season. The clubs don't have the gate money coming in so why should the players be paid the same? I have suggested it to a number of my clubs, but I don't think it will ever come back in. The PFA and the agents would never stand for it.

I sound like an old man looking back, but we had to work during the summer months to supplement our incomes. For example, Don used to be a funeral director, Mike Summerbee and Ernie Hunt went gravedigging and Keith Morgan and I worked in the stores at Wills Tobacco. You wouldn't get that today, players would claim they need their summer break, but we played just as many matches as they do today!

The other thing I would do would be to make sure that players had a real incentive to be in the first team and to play well and win. These days players seem to be able to pick up much the same level of money whether they are in the first team or not, and regardless of how the team is doing the basic wages are too high. Much better to make the pay linked in to how the player, and the team, are doing. At least you're seeing some sense now, with a number of clubs linking basic pay with what Division the team is in, if only that had been in place when Swindon were in the Premiership, a lot of the club's current financial problems wouldn't have happened.'

Contracts are another major change since John's day.

'In my career we only ever had contracts for one year, never longer. You used to go in as a team in the week after the last game of the season and see the manager, and he would tell you if your services were being retained for the following year. It was only towards the end of my career that I had a contract for two years.

I was lucky in that I'd usually played a fair number of games over the season, so I was expecting to be retained, but it could be quite an ordeal for some of the fringe players. There was very little security back then in football. It was only towards the end of my career that I wondered if I would be retained, once you are past 30 you always wonder if they might want to bring in someone younger than you!'

With his appearance record, there was, in truth, little doubt about the club retaining John. He was well liked and respected by those he played under, and his consistency on the pitch ensured a smooth ride off it come contract time. However, there was one occasion when he did come close to leaving over his contract.

'It was during Les Allen's spell as manager, the summer of 1973, I had my annual contract put in front of me and as usual there was a small rise on the table. The problem was that I knew that a number of players had come in and had not only been paid what in those days were pretty good signing-on fees, but were earning more that I was on as a basic wage as well. I began to feel that I was being taken for granted by the club, so I refused to sign.

In the end I was told to go and see the chairman, who was very concerned. He said "hang on John, we can't have you leaving, you're an institution here, what would the fans say?" So I explained my problem about what the newer players were on, which he explained away by saying "that's what we have to pay them to come to Swindon, otherwise they would never sign". Anyway, in the end I got my point of view across, and made them realise that I felt it was unfair not to reward the longer-serving players properly as well, and I got my extra £5 or so a week, which is all I wanted, although £5 was a reasonable sum back then.'

So John has seen many changes. He is not like some 'old pros' who simply think everything was better in 'their day'. He can see benefits in a number of the changes that have happened in football in the last 40 years or so and indeed would take advantage of a number of them in his role as a coach. However, on one thing he is adamant: 'we had more fun in our day' and, somehow, it is impossible not to agree with him.

THE PLAYERS

At a conservative estimate, John played with well over 250 players during his time on the playing staff. He also saw many others pass through the club in his capacity as manager, assistant manager and youth-team coach, and is, therefore, well placed to pass comment on pulling together a 'best ever Swindon XI'. The only criteria is that the player must have represented the club during John's 37 years at the club.

John's team surprised me enormously. Some people who I thought would make it weren't selected, and others he did select were those that perhaps fans might not have gone for. The result makes for an interesting insight into the man himself. We start, unsurprisingly enough, with the goalkeeper. Some of the positions had John debating between a number of players. Not this one though

'It would have to be Peter Downsborough in goal. He was the best shot stopper I ever played with, perhaps not the best at coming off his line, and not the tallest either, but he was just so good at doing what he had to do with the minimum of fuss. He saved us time and time again in the League Cup-winning era, most notably at Wembley, when, without him, the game would have been all over in the first 20 minutes. He was very reliable and very little got past him.

Fraser Digby was somebody who would run him close. He was someone else who served the club very well and wasn't that far behind Peter in the pecking order. Fraser was excellent off his line and had a great build and temperament for a 'keeper, he was an excellent signing by Lou Macari when he joined from Manchester United.

Jimmy Allan was another good 'keeper. Bear in mind that

Swindon had a number of long-serving 'keepers whilst I was at the club. Jimmy was probably just a bit behind the other two, but he was very brave and, like Fraser, came off his line well.'

Those three might be the best goalkeepers in John's eyes, but there is no doubt in his mind as to which goalkeeper he would want in the dressing room.

'If you're talking about goalkeepers, you have to mention Sam Burton, who was definitely the best character, goalkeeper or otherwise, that I played with. He and Maurice Owen, as I've said before, were a dangerous duo. Maurice used to supply the ammunition and Sam used to fire it. My favourite memory of Sam is a game against Birmingham. Their winger, Mike Halliwell, who was a very quick player, got inside me and was running on goal when he heard a whistle and stopped. The referee waved play on. The whistle hadn't come from him but from Sam, who had whistled through his teeth as Mike was bearing down on him, and it had sounded just like the referee's whistle. Of course, Sam acted all innocent and there was nothing the referee could do, he just assumed that it had come from the crowd. He'd never have got away with it now! He also used to do "the windmill" before penalties were taken that he was facing in a bid to distract the kicker – he'd wave his arms round and round. You do miss the characters. As I spend more time in football there are fewer and fewer around, and the game just gets more and more serious, too much at stake I suppose, but you do wish that there was a bit more laughter on the pitch. It should be enjoyed, after all.'

For right-back there is a bit of a debate, with John deliberating a while about who he should choose between Rod Thomas and Terry Wollen. In the end, it's the League Cup winner who gets the vote.

'I've got to plump for Rod, just, partly because of what he achieved in the game – he won Welsh international caps, and he fitted very easily into playing First Division football with Derby County and won a Championship medal with them, so he clearly had talent.

I always thought that Rod found the game very easy. He seemed to stroll though games at time. He was very long-legged and made good use of that. He was the quickest player at the club, which not many people realised, everyone assumed it was Donald, but Rod would beat Don at sprints in training.

Rod wasn't the best of trainers, and was fortunate in that he didn't really have to work at his fitness, he had no weight to carry and could run off any excesses without too many problems.'

It says much, though, for how much John rates Terry Wollen that Wollen pushed Thomas so close, and this despite playing only two seasons in League football.

'I think Terry would have been a really, really good player, and would have been another one of 'Bert's Babes', who would have played at the very top. He was a cracking player: good on the ball, good awareness of where other players were and a good athletic footballer. It was such a shame that his career ended so early, because he could have gone a long way in the game.

Of more modern players, I liked David Kerslake, he was exactly the type of player you wanted at right-back when Glenn Hoddle was playing because he could make good use of those raking balls that Glenn used to play to the flanks. David's ability to cross the ball, particularly with the outside of his foot, was excellent, but I just felt that perhaps he wasn't as good defensively as Rod or Terry.

And so to left-back. Not that he would ever do it, he's much too modest a man for that, but I do stress to John that he cannot pick himself. (I have read books where, much to my irritation, the author does pick themselves in their best ever 11!) The problem is that because John kept the left-back spot for 20 years there are fewer players to choose from. In the end there can only be one winner.

'I thought Paul Bodin was an excellent left-back, he was so cultured on the ball and had this ability to play a superb ball into the penalty area from the wing, either on the run or from a set-piece situation. It took him a while to settle in at Swindon, and I think initially the crowd weren't quite sure what to make of him because he seemed to have so much time on the ball it could look as if he wasn't putting the effort in. However, the crowd soon saw his quality, and he became a firm favourite with them, particularly when he had that one season (1992–93) when he scored a load of goals from left-back, both from the penalty spot and from open play.'

On now to the centre-halves. John is clearly enjoying this and explains his philosophy for selection.

'You have to look at the centre-halves as a pair, really, because how they play together is so important. It's no good, in my view, having two very similar players in that position, ideally you want one ball player and one who is more rugged.'

Having outlined his philosophy, John's choices then follow that thought pattern. Lets start with the more rugged player, for which he has a difficult choice.

'I think there are two players who could play in this position: Frank Burrows and Shaun Taylor. In the end, possibly because I played with him, and saw first hand how important he was to the team, I'll go for Frank, just!

Frank was the final piece in that League Cup-winning side. He was a critical signing. He brought tremendous competitiveness and leadership to the team and to the defence – he would throw himself at anything. He may not have been the best on the ball, but he would run through a brick wall for you, and the impact he had on the rest of the team was huge in many ways. Whilst Stan Harland was the club captain, Frank was our leader on the pitch.

For such a hard player, Frank spent a lot of time on the treatment table, and he was one of those regularly "conned" by Harry Cousins when he was there. Frank used to go in and complain about a problem he had, and Harry used to put something on his leg and then go off and come back 10 minutes later, and take it off. "That will do the trick" Harry would say, and send Frank on his way, with Frank unaware that Harry had done nothing at all, he hadn't switched anything on!'

Frank may have got John's vote – he is clearly a big fan of the Scotsman – but Shaun Taylor runs him very close.

'I thought Shaun did a fantastic job for the club during the early 1990s, and in many ways he was a very similar player to Frank in that he was very brave, very committed and a real leader out on the pitch. He scored a lot of goals as well. He was a superb header of the ball from a set-piece. The only question mark you might have would be about his quality on the ball, which would mean that you probably wouldn't play him with Frank, and so he'd just lose out.'

On now to what John would describe as the 'ball playing' centre-half. Here, for me at least, is the surprise choice in the team, John going for someone who served the club in what was a comparatively unsuccessful period for them, the mid-1970s. His name? Steve Aizelwood.

'I know that people will perhaps do a double-take simply because he wasn't very high-profile as a player, but I was a big fan of Steve. He had a lot going for him as a player, he was good in the air, he had good positional sense and could distribute the ball very well. I thought he underachieved in his career given his talent, and I suspect the main reason for that may well have been the fact that he wasn't a very good trainer at all and perhaps didn't look after himself as well as he could have done.'

It didn't take long for John to make his choice of Aizelwood, but that doesn't mean that he didn't consider others.

'Colin Calderwood was clearly one of the best players Swindon have had in recent years at the back. He was very steady, not the quickest, in fact Jon Gittens used to get him out of a few difficult positions, but he had great positional sense and had a terrific attitude to the game. I suspect many might put him ahead of Steve, but I just feel Steve had more quality on the ball. Mel Nurse would be another contender. He was a very good, ball playing centre-half, and, of course, Stan Harland was another good quality defender, although probably not as good a distributor of the ball as Mel Nurse or Steve. No, Steve it is, he was much underrated as a player to my mind.'

So, that's the defence. On to the midfield. First is the centre-midfield duo, not something that takes much time to select.

'First in would be Ernie Hunt. He had such great ability with the ball. He is probably the best screener of a ball that I've ever seen, you just couldn't get to see the ball once he got it with his back to goal. As we used to say in the dressing room, he had a big arse! In fact I do just wonder whether he was just a bit too well built, and whether that, in fact, shortened his career towards the end. He was another one who enjoyed life off the pitch!

Ernie, of course, was a born joker and would be great in the dressing room of this team, although the joke I associate most with Ernie is one that he was on the wrong end of. It was when he had just come into the team and when Sam Burton was still at the club. We used to change at the old pavilion in Shrivenham Road, and there was a toilet alongside the bath with a vent outside. Anyway, one day, around Bonfire Night, Ernie went to the toilet, and Sam managed to get a firework through the vent, into the cubicle and straight into the toilet pan, where, of course, it exploded just as Ernie was doing his business. You should have seen the state of Ernie when he came out!'

So, who to play alongside Ernie? John considers the options and comes up with a number: John Smith, a teammate in the League Cup-winning side, and, sadly, the first of that side to pass on, Roger Smart, another 1969 hero and 'very underrated' in John's view, John Moncur, an inspired Hoddle signing in the 1990s, and Micky Hazard, like Moncur, part of the promotion-winning side of 1992–93 and another former Tottenham player. However, once John realises that he can choose another member of the promotion-winning side then there is no further debate.

'So can I choose Glenn Hoddle, given that he played when I was at the club, presumably I can? [I nod]. In that case there is no debate, what a player he was, even though he was at the end of his career. That ability to spray the ball around, I've never seen anyone who could do that, before or since, it was just great to watch. He must be one of the most, if not the most, naturally talented footballers England have produced since the war in terms of passing ability, and to think that he played at Swindon – we were very lucky. You couldn't leave him out, could you?'

At this point I make a big mistake. I venture to suggest that perhaps Hunt and Hoddle might not be the most competitive in midfield when it comes to winning tackles, and might John need more of a midfield enforcer. Not a good suggestion.

'I hate the idea of sending out a team and restricting players in what they can do, whether it be going forward, expressing themselves, movement off the ball or playing the game as it should be played. There is just too much today of teams being set up by a manager not to lose and packing the midfield with players who can't really play but can run and tackle – it makes for a terrible game to watch – I mean, some of the games I saw Paul [his son] play in for Bristol Rovers last season were just shocking in terms of entertainment value. I wouldn't want any team I managed playing like that.'

So, two highly creative players in midfield, and given John's footballing philosophy there was never any danger of his other two selections for midfield being anything but orthodox wingers.

'On the left wing it has to be Don Rogers, who I think is probably the best player ever to play for Swindon, certainly one who spent any real length of time at the club. He was a terrific winger and also an incredible goalscorer, when you look at how many goals he scored as a winger it's quite remarkable. Most of this was due to the fact that he was the best one-on-one finisher, along with Jimmy Greaves, that I have ever seen. When he was through on the goalkeeper he had the ability to go past him on either side.

In some ways you can pick holes in Don's game. I mean he couldn't tackle, and for a reasonably big man he was poor in the air, mainly because he didn't put his head in! However, he was very good at doing what he was able to do, and Don in full flight was a wonderful sight. He stayed at Swindon too long. Had he left earlier, I think that he would have played for England.'

The choice of right-winger is more difficult, though, with another surprise as a well-known England international ends up losing to a man who played his career for unfashionable clubs.

'I guess everyone would expect me to select Mike Summerbee because he went on to have such a great career with Manchester City and England. He deserved that success because he was a very good player who was a superb crosser of the ball, and it was obvious when I played with him that he would go on and have real success in the game.

However, I think that Dave Moss was probably a bit more rounded as a player, even though he didn't achieve what Mike did in the game. Dave played on both flanks for Swindon, which shows his versatility, and he could go both inside and outside of players. Like Don, I thought he was good at bringing others into the games. Sometimes wingers can try and do too much, and not involve others enough. I really enjoyed playing with him because I knew that if I made a run then I would have a reasonable chance of getting the ball! He also scored a decent number of goals from the wing, which was another string to his bow.

I think perhaps Dave underachieved in his career. I know he played in the old First Division for Luton, but he could have played for a higher-profile club, I think. Perhaps he stayed at Swindon too long, like Don.'

So, who are the two strikers who will benefit from the chances that the midfield would undoubtedly create? As with the wingers, John makes one choice immediately; the other takes more thought.

'Peter Noble was a wonderful player and a great professional as well. He could hold the ball up very well, which, given the system that the 1969 side played, was important, and for a smaller fellow he was a great header of the ball. He really proved his class when he went to Burnley and played regularly in the First Division. Even there he was viewed by the professionals as one of the most underrated players in the game.

I liked playing with Peter. He was a very unselfish player for you, he wouldn't hide, no matter how the game was going, and he would always show for you and put himself in a position where you could pass to him. In fact, I would often pass to Peter if I couldn't find Don.'

The second striker is more problematic. A number of names are considered: Bronco Layne, with whom John played early on in his career, Jack Smith, another player from the 1960s, Duncan Shearer from the late 1980s and early 1990s, Paul Rideout, the young prodigy given his debut by John while manager, and two players who were good in the air, Dave Bamber and Jimmy Quinn. In the end, though, John, by now taking this very seriously, disregards the latter two players because 'I'd want my team to play with the ball on the floor'. The choice, in the end, is another player who left the County Ground for the First Division, Peter Eastoe.

'Peter was a very good goalscorer and had that happy knack of being in the right place at the right time in and around the box. He wasn't the biggest or the best in the air, but he was bright and lively and his movement was very good. He scored goals for us when we weren't the best team, and I wasn't surprised that he went on to do well in the First Division. He was another good lad to play with as well, a good team player.'

So there we are, the team is selected. To recap, it is:

Downsborough

Thomas	Burrows	Aizelwood	Bodin
Moss	Hoddle	Hunt	Rogers
	Noble	Eastoe	

One final question then: who will the manager be? We have already heard John's views on his managers. In the end he opts for what I diplomatically call a fudge.

'I'll have Danny Williams as manager, but I will back him up with Fred Ford as coach, that way I get the best of both worlds. Danny would be great as a motivator and to keep spirits up round the dressing room, whilst you would have the added benefit of

Fred's organisational skills and coaching ability. I suppose it would be even better than that because I'd also have Glenn Hoddle, who I think was the best tactician I ever saw, on the pitch as well, so I'd get the benefit of his brains in the dressing room. It would be quite a management team.'

So there is the team, one or two shocks in John's selection but with three full internationals and eight players with top flight experience, it does just go to show the quality of some of the players John lined up with during his career. It would certainly be an attacking side, and, as John says, with Danny Williams as the manager the sole priority would be going forward with more focus on scoring goals rather than on making sure goals weren't conceded!

THE MANAGERS

During his time at Swindon, John either played under or worked under a total of 12 managers. While some, like Danny Williams or Bobby Smith, were relatively low profile before they came to Swindon, a number of others, particularly while John was youth-team manager, were anything but low profile.

'I suppose it's inevitable that when you spend as long as I did at one club you are going to see a number of managers come and go. In fact, looking back on it, I suppose it is a surprise that I didn't work with more managers – 37 years is a long time, and I think that in today's game where managers are changed very frequently you would expect to work with a lot more if you had that length of time at a club.

I don't think the current trend of chopping and changing the manager all the time does anybody any good really. It doesn't help the players, who need time to get to know the manager, to get to trust him, and to understand how he wants the game to be played, and it certainly doesn't help the managers, who are under pressure from very early on to deliver results. You don't get the chance, nowadays, to build a club from the bottom. You can understand why some of the current managers don't seem very interested in their youth teams, they know they won't be around to see the kids come through.'

So let's go through the managers. Elsewhere in this book you will find a more factual account of what happened on the pitch during their time at Swindon. This chapter is intended to convey a little more about what they were like as people, coaches and managers, and as men to work with.

First up for John was Bert Head, the man who gave him his first-team debut at 17, and who was in many ways a second father figure to the young, somewhat shy, left full-back who was finding his way in League football back in the early 1960s.

'In the 1950s and 1960s you didn't used to have coaches like you do today. The managers were probably less involved in the day-to-day training, and Bert was no different. He used to leave the training to people like Ellis Stuttard and Jack Connolly. Yet, obviously, he was a huge influence on my career and I can't praise him enough.

Bert was, in some ways, an old-fashioned bloke. He set very high standards both on and off the pitch, and he expected you to live up to those standards. He certainly would not have tolerated the behaviour off the pitch of some of today's young players. He always took the view that what you did away from football had an important impact on how you performed on the pitch. The worst crime in Bert's book was not giving 100 percent, whether in matches or training, and woe betide anyone who he though wasn't fully committed.

You always knew what was expected of you and where you stood – he was very a straight person.'

Head has a reputation for being a strong disciplinarian, but would John agree with that assessment?

'I think Bert was strict, particularly with the young players, and remember he mainly had young players in his team. I certainly got some good old fashioned rollockings from him in my early days, but they were probably deserved. All I know is that when I told my dad that I'd been in trouble with Bert for some reason, my Dad usually agreed with Bert and gave me another rollicking! However, although he was hard, Bert was very fair. He didn't set out to rule with a rod of iron like some managers I could name, where he was deliberately trying to intimidate players. I owe him a lot because the standards that he set gave me a great start in my football career, and because I was taught how to treat football as a career with the respect it needed early on it certainly helped me to play for as long as I did.'

Head will always be associated with 'Bert's Babes', the young Swindon side that did so well in the early 1960s. To what degree does John think that Bert was lucky in having such a talented group of players come together at the same time? In other words, was it a case of right place, right time?

'Yes, Bert was lucky that he had some talented people coming through at the same time, but I still think he deserves enormous credit for what he did. Firstly, he had to have the courage to play the youngsters, and all at the same time as well. It's one thing to blood one or two, which is low risk, but to play an entire team of kids, well that takes some guts. He saw our potential and was prepared to back us. Few managers would have done that. The fact that he backed us and encouraged us then gave us the confidence to do well. You felt that if this tough football man believed enough in you to put you in the first team then you must be good enough.

The other thing that Bert should take great credit for is that he set us all up to have long careers in the game by bringing us up as kids in the right way. Look at the kids he brought in. Most of us played hundreds of League games, from the early youngsters like Keith Morgan through to the likes of Don, Mike Summerbee and Ernie Hunt. Most of that side had good, long careers, and I think a lot of that was down to the good habits picked up under Bert.'

The respect that John has for his first manager is evident when he sums up Head's career.

'Swindon got rid of Bert much too quickly. It is a classic case of a club getting too high expectations really. When he joined the club they had never been promoted and were going nowhere, so if you had said he would get promotion then anyone at the club would have been absolutely delighted. Then, as soon as he got promotion, expectations changed, and people suddenly forgot what a poor state the club was in when he came, and he lost his job. He was treated badly – not only had he got promotion, but he had developed players like Bobby Woodruff, Ernie Hunt, Mike Summerbee and Don Rogers, who made Swindon good money.

Bert was an excellent manager. You only need to look at what he then did at Crystal Palace after leaving Swindon. Had he been given the chance, I am sure he would have got the team promoted again, although whether he would have done it as quickly as Danny is anybody's guess.'

So, on to Danny Williams, the unknown Yorkshireman, who would lead the team to League and Cup glory. John would readily admit that he wasn't sure what to expect when Williams arrived, but there's no doubt that he enjoyed his time with his second manager.

'Danny was much more free and easy, as both a manager and a person, than Bert was. He actively encouraged off-the-cuff play and was much less methodical and disciplined, so he really wasn't into detailed tactics at all. However, he was very good for us as a team because at that stage we needed a boost, and Danny's personality gave us that. He was always happy and jovial and was good to have around the club in that respect. Some managers can be a bit up or down, you never quite know what mood they will be in when you come for training. With Danny you never had that concern, he would always be the same.'

John says he learnt something from most of the people who he played under, and is very clear on what he took from the Williams years, which of course spanned 1974–78, as well as the more successful 1965–69 spell.

'Danny was very good at focusing on people's strengths rather than their weaknesses, and letting people express themselves on the pitch. For example, it was under him that I really started to overlap, and Danny encouraged me to do that because he could see I enjoyed it and had the energy to get up and down the pitch. He was the same when talking about the opposition. He wasn't that interested in them. He used to tell us to worry about what we did, not what the opposition did, and to play the way we wanted to do, so they had to adapt to us rather than we to them.'

Sometimes that philosophy could be taken a little to extremes, John explains when recalling a game at Huddersfield.

'Danny was doing his teamtalk, and as usual he had his notes on the opposition, such that they were, written down on scraps of paper and the back of cigarette packets. Anyway, he came to me and started to read out about Dick Kryzwicki, the Huddersfield winger, who I was marking. Clearly the scout had rated him because Danny was telling me how good he was. Anyway, he got to the end of telling me what he had written down and then stopped. "PTO" he said, "what does that mean, PTO?" The lads were in stitches because Danny was genuinely confused. Then the door opened and the teamsheets came in, and Danny said "don't worry John, Kryzwicki isn't playing, he's injured." Apparently, this had been known well beforehand!'

So, what was Williams's greatest asset? John is very clear on that.

'Danny was a great team builder. The sad thing is that if he were managing today I don't think he'd get the time to do what he did back in the 1960s and 1970s. What he did was great, it wasn't just that he bought good players, often players who no one had heard of, but he was able to see how they would blend together into a team. He did his research as well, that team of 1969 had some of the best professionals that I played with in terms of their attitude to the game and their willingness to work for their teammates. As a result, I think in some ways the League Cup-winning team ran itself from a footballing point of view, we all knew our jobs and didn't need great tactical input from Danny.

He did the same thing again when he came back in the 1970s. This time, perhaps, he didn't get the same success, but he laid the foundations of the side that Bobby Smith took to the League Cup semi-final in 1980.'

John has one overwhelming memory of playing under Williams.

'It was fun, both on and off the pitch. Looking back, as the records show, other than the 1969 side we weren't great defensively, in fact, quite the reverse, but Danny never minded that, he just wanted us to entertain and score goals, and we certainly did that.'

After Williams moved, for what would be an unsuccessful spell in South Yorkshire, Fred Ford took over as John's third boss in what was his 10th year as a professional. Again, the respect John has is very clear.

'Fred Ford was the best coach I played under. He was very organised and good at making training interesting. You felt you were developing as a professional when you listened to him and did the routines he'd put together. It was hard to follow Danny, but Fred did it and was much respected among the team. He was hard working, always at the club, morning, noon and night.'

The team also had their fair share of laughs at Fred's expense.

'As Don said in his book, Fred only had three fingers on one of his hands, and we always used to take the mickey out of him when he told us he wanted "four in the wall" and then held up three fingers to demonstrate! We also enjoyed it in the Anglo-Italian Cup when, after lecturing us not to eat the fruit or drink the water, Fred didn't take his own advice, and was the only one of us to get ill. Not that you'd laugh in front of Fred mind. He had a very quick temper – on more than one occasion he pinned players up against the dressing room wall when he was annoyed about something.'

Next was Dave Mackay, the first 'big name' to manage John. Head, Williams and Ford weren't even household names in their own houses, as the saying goes, when they arrived at the County Ground. Mackay was different, he arrived with a playing record that warranted huge respect. In many ways he was the most well-known player ever to play for the club when he arrived in 1971. John would recognise his abilities as a footballer, but was less sure about him as a manger.

'We all had enormous respect for what Dave had done as a player. He had been a great player in his time, although by the time he came to us his best days were behind him. As a manager, though, I wasn't so sure. It didn't help him that a lot of the players were very unhappy with the way in which his appointment came about. We were all fond of Fred and felt he was badly treated, which I accept wasn't necessarily down to Dave, although you do wonder about the politics.

As a manager, I wasn't sure he had a lot to offer. All we did was five a sides, and you had the feeling sometimes you were doing the games because Dave enjoyed them. We did ask him why we played so many five a sides and his response was that it was because that's what all the top clubs did for training, which I'm not sure was right for us. I can accept it was difficult for him because he'd been such a great player, and felt that everyone else should be at his standard, but the truth is that we weren't, and we needed to be coached and trained in a way that reflected that. The truth is that on the coaching and the tactical side he had little to offer the players, and we suffered as a result. I'm not sure he was always the best judge of players whilst he was at Swindon really, one or two of the players he brought in weren't as good as we'd been used to.'

If this sounds harsh, John is keen to recognise that, although Mackay's time at Swindon didn't work out, it didn't prevent him from going on to having success elsewhere.

'I think some of the things I've said reflect the fact that this was his first management job. When he took over I'm not sure he had a great knowledge of management or coaching, but clearly he learned from his time at Swindon because he went on to do very well at Derby later on, and I'm sure he developed his approach as he got more experience.'

After Mackay, who was only manager for a year, left, Swindon brought in another man who had played at the top level, Les Allen.

'Les Allen was another man whose playing career meant that he started off with respect from the players, which always helps. However, as many managers have shown, having been a good player doesn't necessarily make you a good manager, and vice versa, and Les's time with us was very unsuccessful.

As a bloke, I got on very well with him, even when he dropped me. He was a very nice bloke. Perhaps he wasn't strong enough though because he listened too much to his assistant, Gordon Eddlestone, who, as you already know, I didn't get on with or rate at all. I'm not sure that Gordon helped Les because he did rub up some of the players the wrong way, and we were looking for Les to help us out, instead of which he backed Gordon and seemed to make decisions based on Gordon's say so.

The other thing about Les was that I'm not sure about his judgement of players. I had got used to playing with a certain quality of players, and I just felt that some of the players that he brought in were nowhere near good enough. He signed a couple from his old club, Queens Park Rangers, and you just wondered whether that link, either consciously or unconsciously, influenced his decisions.'

Danny Williams returned after Allen was sacked in February – a welcome return from John's perspective, who commented that 'He was still the same Danny'. As before, Williams led a side that was very good going forward but not so good defensively. 'We never practised defending' says John.

Next would be an unknown manager, Bobby Smith. By now John was on the coaching staff, having been appointed youth-team manager in the last days of Danny Williams's reign, although, as we have seen, he would return to first-team playing duties under the new manager.

'I'd never heard of Bobby Smith before he arrived, and I hadn't heard of Wilf Tranter, who was his assistant, either. Bobby was very young when he was appointed (in fact he was younger than John) but soon made a good impression. I was particularly pleased that he took the youth team so seriously. Of all the managers I worked with, he had the most interest in that side of the club.

As a manager, he was very good organisationally, and he brought in some of the more "modern" ways of doing things into the club, like doing a pre-match warm-up for example. He was very hard-working and the players liked and respected him.

I felt things started to go wrong for Bobby when Wilf Tranter left for business reasons. Wilf was very popular with players, but his replacement, Dennis Butler, was much less respected, mainly because he was much more abrasive and difficult to deal with. Then Bobby started to sign "big name" players, who of course wanted big money, both wages and signing-on fees, to come to Swindon, and this had an impact on team spirit. For example, it became known in the dressing room that David Peach was on nearly double what the other players were on, which didn't go down at all well and had a bad impact on team spirit.

I don't blame Dave Peach at all, he was offered the money and took it, but there is no doubt in my mind that it was an error of judgement by Bobby. He'd done very well by signing players like Alan Mayes and Andy Rowland, who were players on the way up, so why he decided to sign players who were perhaps on their way down, I don't know. The team spirit was never the same again, and that led to poor results and Bobby losing his job, which was a shame because he was a good bloke to work and play for, and he'd done very well in his first 18 months or so at the club.'

Bobby Smith's departure led to John taking over, and then, after John was relieved of his duties, his assistant, Ken Beamish, took over. Beamish had been brought to the club by John, and John returned to his old job as youth-team manager as had been agreed. It was, therefore, a rather odd situation where John found himself reporting in to somebody who he had only recently been the boss of.

'I thought Ken did all right really. I know the results weren't very good, but you have to remember that the financial situation was absolutely appalling, so he couldn't do much in terms of spending any money. He was a decent enough coach, but I felt he let himself down, a bit like Bobby Smith had done, in his choice of assistant. He brought in Paul Richardson, who was like a bull in a china shop, always losing his temper and bawling at the players, which didn't help make things any better.'

Beamish departed at the end of the 1983–84 season. His replacement was the first of three managers who would put Swindon back on the footballing map, Lou Macari.

'Lou led by example really. He was as fit as a fiddle, and he was so enthusiastic in everything he did it couldn't help but rub off on the players. I have to say I found him great. He was a super fellow.

Lou had strong principles regarding football, and he was very clear about the way in which he wanted you to play: second ball was key, and he wanted to "play in their half", which meant lots of long balls and knock downs. That meant players had to be fit, and there was a huge focus on running in training. The players did some running every day, and some of the runs would be as long as 5 miles, which came as a huge shock to some of the team!

Lou was a gambler, of course, and the team he built also had some gamblers in people like Dave Bamber, Chris Kamara and Peter Coyne. On away trips, they'd bet on anything, for example, what the next advert would be on the television!

He was also a firm disciplinarian. He used to enjoy taking the lads to army camps as part of the fitness campaign, and I recall going to Tidworth Army Camp one year pre-season. We played a friendly at Salisbury, and Lou let the players out until midnight and went to bed, but told Kevin Morris, the physio, and I to check them back in. Around 1am some of the players were still out, and we were just sat there waiting for them, when we heard a lot of laughter. It was a group of players trying to get back in through the window. The noise woke Lou, who was absolutely furious and came down to send them home at 1am in the morning with no transport! We all tried to calm him down and wait until morning to pack them off, but Lou wouldn't back down, and in the end it was only some hard lobbying by Colin Calderwood, who was the captain, that meant Lou relented and let them stay the night before sending them back home in the morning.

He was very strict in the things he believed in. Another example would be him making players come back from away trips if they hadn't played and run at the County Ground!

As I say, I was a big fan of Lou as a person, even though I didn't see eye to eye with him in terms of football philosophy. I suppose the one criticism you might make of him was around his fixed style of play – he was resolute in always having the same tactics. If you look at what happened to him later on in his management career, especially at the bigger clubs like Celtic and West Ham, you just wonder whether the better players appreciated his tactics, or, in fact, if they worked at a higher level. The other issue would be around his lack of willingness to play the younger players. He tender to buy, rather than to bring, players through, even though we had some good youngsters at Swindon towards the end of his time there, like Paul Hunt, Fitzroy Simpson, Adie Viveash and Nicky Summerbee.'

Macari resigned in the summer of 1989 having taken the club to the very brink of the top flight of English football, a remarkable achievement given that he inherited a club who had just finished 17th in the basement Division just five years earlier. His replacement, also as player-manager, was another famous player – Argentinian World Cup winner Ossie Ardiles. The two men were very different.

'Ossie was all about playing football, I think probably at times too much football. He was great at getting the players to play little triangles all over the park, and he positively hated any long balls because he was so keen on keeping possession. It was great for me as a youth coach because the way he had the first team playing was one the youngsters couldn't help but learn from.

As a bloke, he was quite quiet really, and his English wasn't great so he tended to leave a lot of the talking in the dressing room to others. His favourite phrase was "play, play, play!" I remember when Fitzroy Simpson got into the first team and played on the wing near the dugouts, he told me that all he could hear was Ossie saying "play Fitz, play!"

Ossie also liked his full-backs to go forward. I think I'd have enjoyed playing under him! Again, you'd be sat next to him on the bench and the right full-back, Dave Kerslake, would be going forward, and Ossie would be shouting at Paul Bodin, our left full-back to, "go Paul, go!" In other words, to get up in the attack. He really liked the players to express themselves, and in some ways when you look back you realise what a good side Lou left him because the same players who had played the long ball under Lou were able to adapt to playing a very different style of football under Ossie. Perhaps, with the benefit of hindsight, Lou didn't trust them enough to express their own creativity, whereas Ossie did.

The one thing that I think caught Ossie out was his lack of focus on physical fitness. We never did any running at all, it was all ballwork. Talk about from one extreme to the other after Lou! You do need some fitness though, and Ossie just didn't do it. He expected players to keep themselves fit, which I think is unrealistic really.'

After Ardiles came another former Tottenham hero, Glenn Hoddle. Once again the emphasis was on footballing skill.

'Glenn was just an awesome footballer, his ability to ping passes out to the two full-backs from the centre of the pitch was incredible. He blended the best of Lou and Ossie from a footballing philosophy: try and play football but be prepared to mix up short passes with long passes if that's the right ball to play.

He was, in many ways, ahead of his time as a manager. He brought in a lot of ideas having worked with Wenger at Monaco, both how to look after your body, like the breathing exercises I mentioned earlier, and also the use of a sweeper and two attacking full-backs. Tactically, in the dressing room he was the best manager I've ever seen, just a great ability to read a game and to make adjustments. That's difficult enough to do from the dugout, but when you're out there playing and trying to focus on your own performance that takes some talent.

I know Glenn has a bit of a reputation for being aloof, but I didn't find that to any great extent. Sure, you'd never call him happy-go-lucky – you'd see him and he'd appear a bit pre-occupied – but he was always fine with me, although we were never close. He relied a lot on John Gorman, who was a superb number two for him in that he was always friendly, cheerful and happy and someone in whom the players felt they could confide. Perhaps Glenn relied on him too much, in that had John not been there Glenn might have had to have got closer to the players, and that might have made for better relationships. I wouldn't say that he had bad relationships with them, but he was never close, even allowing for the distance that you need as a manager.'

What might Swindon have done in the Premier League had Hoddle stayed as manager after promotion in 1993 is anybody's guess. In the event, they played their one and only season in the top flight under Gorman, who was appointed manager after Hoddle left for Chelsea.

'I don't think that John should have been appointed manager, and I mean that in the most positive way because I am very fond of the man. John was just such a good number two, so good with the players, so bubbly and friendly, that I think that was his niche in football. As a manager he couldn't be as close to players, which was his great strength, and, of course, he faced a huge job from the start by taking on his first management job in the Premier League.

I don't think that he helped himself by appointing Andy Rowland as his number two, although I'm not sure it was completely his decision to do so. I felt that as a young, inexperienced manager taking on a Premier League job, with a team that had never played there, he needed someone who had been there and done it as his assistant, so he had someone to turn to when times were tough. He tried to play football all the time. If you look back then Swindon played some great football in that season, despite the results, whereas perhaps with a more experienced staff around him John might have been persuaded to have sacrificed some of his purist footballing principles for results.'

Finally, we come to Steve McMahon. You won't, having read the account of how John was treated by the former Liverpool and England player, expect John to be too complimentary. He's not.

'When Steve first came to the club I didn't think I'd have a problem with him, although I knew that I wouldn't be close to him because he wasn't my type of person. He wasn't interested in the youth team or the centre of excellence at all. He rarely came to watch, and if he did he would never stay for the full game.

I just found him an abrasive person. His man-management throughout the club, other than with his own people, who he gradually got into the club, was very poor. He would just ignore people in the club at times. He always struck me as a very angry man. I don't know why because he'd had a very good career as a player.

There were things that used to wind him up for no apparent reason, like anyone talking about what had happened under Glenn or Lou, or, even worse, what had happened in 1969. He used to hate that. I wonder if he felt threatened by success the club had enjoyed before he came.

As his power in the club increased, in that second season when the team won promotion he just became more and more difficult to deal with and used his power to bring in his friends, and I was one of the people who suffered. I don't have any time for him as a bloke, and I don't think he was a great manager either, as has subsequently been proved by the fact that he didn't do much at Blackpool once he'd left Swindon.'

Overall, John is complimentary about his managers. Having done the job himself, he is well qualified to talk about the way in which each of his bosses conducted themselves. He clearly has great affection for most of those he played or worked under; it is just a shame that the story of the managers finishes on a low note.

'I do consider myself fortunate, really. To have played and worked under some of the people I did is quite an honour. If you look back, I only had any real problem with a couple of people as blokes [Gordon Eddlestone and Steve McMahon] and a couple of others as managers [Dave Mackay and Les Allen]. When you consider some of the stories from other players I knew who moved on from Swindon, and their tales of the managers they played under, I think I was very, very lucky.

THE FAMILY VIEW

I've spent the last few months listening to John's story and living his career through his own eyes. I've spoken to those who knew him in a footballing context, but I need to know more about the man, and who better to ask than his family: his wife of over 40 years, Maureen, and his two children, Sara and Paul. So, on a glorious summer evening, I drive the short distance back to Highworth to meet them and to try and find out more about John the family man.

The obvious person to start with is Maureen. How did she and John meet?

'I first met John was I was 10 and he was 11. He was captain of the Wroughton Junior School football team, and he came to play football at the school I was at in Highworth – he was very shy! We started going out when I was 17. He was surrounded by girls at McIlroys in Swindon, and I decided to go and ask him to dance. He said yes and that was the start of it – not that we've done much dancing since.

I've had football in the blood from an early age. My dad was a local footballer, and we used to watch him in all manner of weather. Then, one of my cousins was Mick Woolford, who was on Swindon's books as a youngster, although he didn't make it. I used to love watching Swindon, although because I was a hairdresser I used to work on Saturday afternoons so I could only go midweek.'

John and Maureen married in the summer of 1965, and, almost immediately, they were faced with a difficult decision. It says much for John's modesty that it is Maureen, and not him, who tells me of an approach from a First Division Club.

'There was always talk of some of the top clubs being interested in John, and the papers used to have headlines saying that so and so "wanted" John Trollope, which was a bit unsettling for me because I was thinking that we might have to move. I remember Everton being one team in particular who were rumoured to be interested in him, although there was never any formal approach that we knew of. However, one night there was a knock on our door and there was a scout for another First Division club, which I won't name, offering John £6,000 if he would sign for his club. Now, to put this into perspective, we'd just bought our bungalow, and it had cost us £2,700, and we'd bought a new car, a Mini, for £300, so this was a lot of money to us. Neither of us wanted to move though, so we turned it down. It was obviously an illegal approach anyway, but that was the way that things used to happen.'

So John stayed and eventually went on to play at Wembley in the League Cup Final, a day that Maureen remembers well.

'There were three players' wives who were pregnant watching the game. I was one of them because I was expecting Sara. I was only five months pregnant though, not as bad as Ann Butler, Joe's wife, who had a suitcase under her seat because she was so close to giving birth. What I do remember is that the pitch was even worse in real life than it looks on the television pictures of the match – it was like a ploughed field. I have no idea why they had allowed the Horse of the Year show to take place on the pitch, although there is no doubt that the conditions helped Swindon.

My other main memory of the game is on the Sunday. All the players and their families watched the match on ATV, as it was then, at The Goddard Arms, and then the players went in buses to take them to the town hall for a reception. The problem was that nobody had remembered about the transport for the wives – in the end we had to get a fleet of taxis.'

Maureen is keen to distance herself from any similarities with today's 'footballer's wives', either those in real life or those portrayed in the television series of the same name.

'We didn't have the same profile as some of them have today. Even at the grounds there was no area for us, just a small tea bar where we used to go and get a drink at half-time. It was fun though, I'm sure more fun than it is today, and we used to have some good laughs. One of the best times was when Eric Morecambe turned up at the County Ground as a Director of Luton Town and ended up spending half an hour with the wives. He had us in absolute stitches.

The only other time that we saw celebrities was in the summer. The football club had a cricket side, and we used to play against a showbiz XI, people like Dennis Waterman and Bill Oddie played. Paul was only little then, and he couldn't believe that he was meeting one of the Goodies, who were very famous back then. He kept running round and round Bill!'

For Paul and Sara football was a large part of their childhood. Maureen used to take them to watch the home games, and, although they are too young to remember much in the way of individual games, Paul was 8 and Sara, 11 when John retired, they can both recall seeing dad play. In Sara's words:

'It was just part of growing up. It was what my dad did, and I never knew anything different, so, for example, you just accepted that he wouldn't be around for some, or even a large part, of Christmas Day because he would be training or travelling to a game on Boxing Day.'

In Paul's case, seeing his dad on the pitch was an inspiration.

'I remember watching him play and thinking that's what I want to do, and being very proud when he used to give us a wave when he was warming up, just before kick-off. We always used to sit in the same place in the old North Stand so he knew where to look for us.'

How about the day that John broke the record? What can his family remember about that? Maureen recollects:

'It went by in a blur really, but everyone was very kind, and we got loads of telegrams and cards congratulating him, and the directors did a presentation as well. He went on to the pitch through a guard of honour. Then he got given his PFA Merit Award, and it was on the television, and I was desperately trying to keep Paul and Sara awake so they could see him receive the award.'

Sara says that it was the gifts of the fans that John appreciated the most.

'He always had a good relationship with the fans. They appreciated what he did for the club, and I know he was very proud when "The Town Enders" presented him with a silver salver for his loyal service – that really got to him.'

Paul cannot remember the night of the record being broken, but says that as a professional footballer himself he now appreciates more than ever before how remarkable the achievement was.

'In order to play that many games you have to have two things going for you. Firstly, you need to be very fit and to have looked after yourself, because, let's face it, to play nearly 800 League games you are going to need to have 20 years in the game. You cannot play professional football for 20 years if you aren't disciplined about fitness. Then, secondly, you need to be a very good player because you need to keep your form over a long period of time, and also be good enough to appeal to a lot of different managers, and, believe me, having played the game that's not easy! I don't think the record will ever be broken, and it's great to think that it's my dad who holds it.'

After playing came his opportunity as first-team manager. John has said that he didn't enjoy this part of his time in football. Nor did his family, as Maureen explains.

'That was a difficult time for us all really. I think it put us all under stresses and strains. I know John was advised not to do the job, but when he told me he was going to do it I supported him because it was a good opportunity. It was all right to start with, but then, when the results went against him, the abuse was just terrible. We had to go ex-directory because of some of the phone calls we were getting. I just felt it was so unfair because the fans just didn't know how bad the financial position was that the club was operating under. There was no money at all for anything: overnight stays, lunches before the game, nothing. And to think that John ran the marathon to raise funds for the club and the fans still gave him stick. It still makes me cross.'

Sara was now at secondary school and found out how cruel children could be.

'Early on, when dad was manager, things were good because he kept them up in that first season and did really well. However, once things started to go wrong I got a lot of stick from classmates who knew that my dad was the Swindon manager, and it was quite nasty really. To be fair to him though, I don't remember him changing at home. He didn't seem to bring the stresses of the job home to us as children.'

John returned to coaching the youngsters, which as Maureen rightly says is his 'forte and his passion'. A few years into the role, he would have a new, young, eager footballer to coach, his own son.

'Dad had really left me alone to enjoy my football until I was 13 or 14. I'd been encouraged to go and watch the youth team and the reserves, but he just let me get on with things. As I got older, he used to do some coaching with me and another lad who went to Swindon, Liam Dixon, at the Rec in Highworth, and teach us more about the game: how to pass, how to get our positional sense right, that sort of thing.

Anyway, I ended up playing under dad in the youth team. That was hard. I don't think I realised at the time how much was being said about me behind my back by some of the apprentices who had joined the club from outside the area, accusing me of only being there because of my dad. The local youngsters were fine because I'd grown up with a lot of them, it was just a small minority really.

Understandably, I guess, so as to make sure he wasn't showing signs of favouritism, I always felt that he was particularly hard on me. If nothing was said to me then I knew I'd had a pretty decent game, otherwise I would be criticised, just like everybody else, perhaps more so!'

Paul then recounts one tale that he is particularly keen makes this book. It is the story of a match while he was playing for the youth team with John as the boss.

'I can't remember now who it was against, but we played one game and I had an absolute stinker. I couldn't do anything right. Anyway, Dad didn't speak to me from after the game until the following Tuesday, and remember I was living at home with him at that time, all through the Sunday if he saw me he just shook his head, then all the way into training on the Monday he just didn't speak to me! We laugh about it now, but at the time it was tough – just an indication of the standards he set.'

Maureen agrees that it was tough for her son.

'There were times when I told them to pack it in because they were often arguing about what had happened in a particular game. It was tough for Paul because he had no escape really, and he suffered a little bit from John's desire to make him the best player he could be. Looking back at Paul's career though, it hasn't worked out that badly has it?'

Paul agrees that although his time under John was tough, it prepared him well for professional football.

'I owe a lot to dad, really, both as my dad and as a coach, because he instilled some really good habits in me that enabled me to have the career I've had. I know I wasn't the absolute best footballer there is, but I have been able to make the most of what I've got through following dad's advice, particularly around dedication to the game, professionalism and fitness. I still talk to him all the time about my game and my career, and he has always given me great advice.'

There is no doubt that John was tough on his charges while he was manager of the youth team. Some of them now wish they had taken some of his advice, as Sara explains.

'I still see a number of the players who used to be under dad when I'm out in town, and many of them have come to me and said that they wished they'd taken more notice of what he was saying when he was youth coach because then they might have done better in the game. I think he was hard on them, but it was for a reason, and they just didn't understand or appreciate it when they were youngsters.'

So, how would his wife and children describe John Trollope the man? Maureen had the following to say about her husband:

'He's changed quite a bit over the 40-odd years I've known him. He used to be really shy, and when we went out with others he'd hardly say anything. He still doesn't like being recognised or having a fuss made over him, but as he's got older he has become much less introverted, and now will give his opinion on things, when he thinks it's needed. Management changed him I think. He is hugely loyal and committed, he gives a lot and expects a lot in return and sets very high standards, for himself and others, but at the same time you can have a really good laugh with him once he realises that you are OK.'

Sara says there are ways in which she is like her father.

'He tends to weigh people up, trying to work out what their character is, so he can come over as quite quiet until people get to know him. However, once he's comfortable with someone he's very different, he relaxes and becomes a different person really. He will certainly call a spade a spade, which some people can find difficult at first, until you realise that he is simply being honest, and, in his book, there is nothing worse than saying one thing and thinking another. I'm very similar like that!'

Paul paints a similar picture.

'How would I describe dad? Loyal, hard-working, dedicated, much the same in his private life as he was on the football pitch really. He's quite a private man, really. He doesn't like the limelight, and is at his happiest when he is with his close friends and family who he can trust – he doesn't like hangers-on really.'

So, there we are. The family group of John, Maureen, Sara and Paul, and not forgetting Paul's wife, Grace, and John's three grandchildren, Eleanor, Chloe and Bayley, is a happy and settled one, and what is evident is the affection in which John is held and also the pride that the family feel over what he's achieved. As Paul says, 'it's an incredible achievement and one that I don't think will ever be beaten.'

THE PROFESSIONAL'S VIEW

So, what was John like to play and work with? Time to find out. My search takes me to talk to three of the League Cup-winning side: Don Rogers, Frank Burrows and Peter Downsborough, who between them played over 1,000 games with John, and also to Lou Macari, the man who restored Swindon's fortunes so spectacularly as a club, and who made John his assistant manager.

Don Rogers

If you want to know about John Trollope, Don Rogers is the person to ask. The two men played over 400 League and Cup games for Swindon together, with Don on the left wing, and John at left-back. Off the pitch they were good friends too, with the two of them and their respective wives regularly socialising together.

'When I made my debut John was the left-back. He is a couple of years or so older than me, and he was established in the team when I first started playing in the League. He was very good to me early on, just helping me settle in, and then over the years we developed a really great understanding. He knew where I liked the ball, and I would play a ball into space for him without having to look. I just knew he would be there.

Down the years he spent most of his time running past me, either up to join the attack or then running back to get back into position! He was a great attacking full-back, in fact we used to joke that if he had been a great finisher he would have been the club's top scorer. I'm sure that some seasons he put more crosses in that I did!

He was very quick and very reliable. You knew that you would get the same level of performance from him each week. He was underrated too. He could easily have played in the First Division. He had the talent and the temperament to handle it, no question about it. However, I think in today's game he would have done even better. He would have been a major star because he would have made a brilliant wing-back. There are few players today who can get up and down a flank like John, and, with his ability to both attack and defend, he would have been ideal for any team that played with wing-backs.

He was a good coach, too, even now I talk to parents whose sons played at Swindon under him but didn't make it, and they tell me how much they appreciated what John did for their kids. He cared about them, and he instilled good habits in them which they could then take on, not just in football but in life too. I enjoy watching him coach. He knows what he is doing, is very confident, and you can see people responding to him. In fact, I was on the phone to him only this week because I want him to do some coaching with my eight-year-old grandson. I cannot think of anyone better to teach the basics.

How he was treated at Swindon at the end was terrible. It really reflects badly on the club because the directors should have had the bottle to stop it happening and didn't. John lost his job because of one man, not because he wasn't doing a good job, and it should never have happened.

John and I have always been close. We roomed together for 10 years, and then most Thursday's before a match he and I, with our wives, used to go out together. It would be frowned on now. We used to have a couple of pints and then a bag of chips to finish the evening, but it didn't seem to do us much harm, did it?

As a man, John is one of the very best. He's quite quiet, especially until you get to know him, but he is fiercely loyal and conscientious and as reliable as they come. If you knew you had something difficult to do you'd want him with you because you know he'd support you all the way and would get things done.

As you can tell, I am a big fan of his, both on and off the pitch. It's nice that this book is being written because I don't think he's ever quite had the accolades he deserves for what he achieved in the game. To play so many games for one club is remarkable. I don't think the record will be broken, and I certainly hope it isn't.'

Peter Downsborough

The Halifax born goalkeeper is now back in his native Yorkshire and remains a good friend of John's. He is well placed to given an opinion on both the man and the player. On the pitch he played over 300 games with John, and off the pitch he and John socialised regularly.

'I thought John was a great player, in many ways very underrated, because what he did, he did without any fuss, so some people may not have seen exactly how well he was playing. Defensively he read the game very well, which was half the battle really. His positional sense was very good, and that, coupled with the fact that he was much quicker than people gave him credit for, meant that he was very rarely caught out.

Of course, he will be best remembered for the understanding he had with Don. They had such a great way of playing together, and in fact part of Don's success was down to the fact that he and John worked so well together. I always thought that whoever signed Don should also sign John, that way you would get the most out of both of them. John allowed Don to play his own game down the left wing because Don knew that John would cover for him defensively and would also support him going forward.

John was a real team man. He would play anywhere for the team, even centre-half. [At this point I remind Peter that John did indeed have one game up front – Peter had forgotten!] He would always put the team first and was very loyal, both to his teammates and also to the club more generally.

He could certainly have played at a higher level, and I suppose I am surprised that he didn't move on. I suppose he was just keen not to uproot his young family, and he was also very settled in the area. He was a real Swindon boy. I think he would have done well had he moved on. Just like some of the other members of that League Cup-winning team were successful in the First Division, John would have been the same.

John and I always got on well. I remember that we both started off playing golf at the same time, and as beginners we went round the course together. We both had terrible problems early on with slicing the ball from the tee. Now, I'm left handed, and John is right handed, so the balls were going everywhere; I remember one lady saying to us that we couldn't like each other much because we only ever met up on the green! Another time we were playing at the Swindon Golf Club, and there was one hole across a valley with the tee being on raised ground. Anyway, John teed off, but it was the club, and not the ball, which flew across this valley – it slipped out of his hand.

As a bloke, John has always been a good friend. I think the thing that sticks out about him is the fact that he is very genuine – one of the most genuine people I ever met in football. He is very loyal and honest. If John says he will do something then it happens, although, like in his football, he will do it quietly and efficiently. He deserves as much recognition as he can get, not that he will like that, because there aren't many people like him.

Frank Burrows

I first met Frank last year when writing a previous book on Don Rogers, and, as then, he is very happy to meet up near his Midlands base to talk about a man for whom he clearly has a lot of respect.

'I knew about John when I joined the club in 1968 because his consistency was well known throughout football. However, the second game that I played for the club was at Hartlepool where he broke his arm and was then out of action for a while.

I saw then what a good professional he was because he couldn't get back in the team. The defence, with Owen Dawson playing at right-back and Rod Thomas moving across to left-back, was very solid and was hardly conceding any goals. It couldn't have been very easy for him because he had been such an automatic choice for so long, but he came in and trained without any fuss and just focused on making himself available for selection. I was very impressed with his attitude.

When he came back, and I started to play with him regularly, I saw what a good player he was. He was naturally very fit and athletic, and was absolutely stunning going forward. Over the years he worked very hard at his defensive game, particularly at defending one on one with wingers. He learnt how to get lower down when facing someone running at you, and he grew in confidence in that aspect of his game.

I think part of the issue for John was that he had been at Swindon for so long that he was taken a bit for granted, and he didn't get the recognition that he deserved. People used to say "Oh yes John Trollope at left-back – Mr Swindon, Mr Reliable" and didn't see what a quality player he was. He could have played in the First Division, there's no doubt about it.

His link up play with Don played an important part in the success of the team that had such a good run in the late 1960s and early 1970s – they had a great understanding. Don was able to hold the ball up so well, and John's ability to run into space meant they created a lot of goals down that left hand flank. John was also clever enough to vary his runs. Once teams got used to him running outside Don he switched his runs so he came inside. I think he got better as he got older. His fitness helped of course, together with his attitude to the game, but he also read the game very well so his positional sense was excellent. Make no mistake about it, John Trollope was a very, very good player.

As a bloke, he was always his own man. He would say his bit in the dressing room when it needed to be said but was generally quite quiet, although he got louder as he got older. He was never swayed by the crowd though. If John wanted to do something he did it, if he didn't, he didn't! I respect him enormously though as both a player and a person. The fact that he holds the record is a reflection of what a loyal and dedicated man he is.'

Lou Macari

I'm fortunate in that I have got to know Lou Macari's cousin, also called Lou Macari, well through a mutual friend, and, therefore, getting to THE Lou Macari is relatively straightforward. Lou Macari senior is helpful and friendly. He clearly has a lot of affection for John.

'I didn't know John before I came to Swindon in 1984, but obviously I knew of him because of the number of games that he played for the club – an unbelievable number. At the time I assumed that anybody who had played that number of games must be focused, dedicated and successful at their job. You cannot spend that long playing football without being those things. I soon learned that John Trollope, the man, was all those things. He was, in many ways, as I expected him to be, based on what he had done during his career.'

Macari, as we have seen, took time to mould the team into playing the way he wanted, and his first season at the club only started to take off towards the end of the campaign. He also had to deal with off-field problems as his relationship with his assistant, Harry Gregg, deteriorated. After Gregg left the club, and Macari, after initially losing his job, was reinstated, the Scotsman needed a new assistant. He chose John.

'I'd worked with John for a few months and I'd seen his qualities, both as a coach and as a person, and I thought he would be an ideal foil to me. Of course, you never get a completely ideal assistant as a manager – there are always things that an assistant does that you'd like them to do differently – but I thought John and I worked well together. We complemented each other, for example, John was, and I'm sure still is, very methodical and very disciplined, so if he says training starts at 2pm, then it will start at 2pm, whereas I'm a bit more harem-scarem; if I say 2pm it could be anytime up to 2.20pm! However, we both put a lot of stall on the fitness side of the game and the importance of working hard, so the players got the message from both of us consistently, which was important.'

John has openly said that he preferred working with younger players, and indeed has recounted the story of Macari saying that this was his

strength. Nearly 20 years since the pair worked together, does Lou still support his original judgement?

'Definitely. John was made to coach younger players. He was absolutely great with them. I think the job of youth coach is the hardest job in football. You've got to be able to coach them as footballers, but it's a difficult time in their lives as well, so you have to watch what happens off the pitch as well. John was excellent at both jobs. He instilled good habits in them but also looked out for them off the pitch as well.

He did a good job at first-team level as well, but I think he found that more difficult, mainly because of the attitude of some of the players. You've got to remember that John as a player was exceptionally fit, exceptionally dedicated and exceptionally focused. Most players don't have that attitude, and I know that John found that frustrating and found it hard to relate to sometimes, and, on the other side, some of the players couldn't understand how he could be so dedicated. I think he felt that, as professional footballers, they should all live their lives, both on and off the pitch, as he did, and it wasn't going to be the case. Perhaps he could have done better with the senior players if he'd been a bit more lenient from time to time.'

So how would Lou sum up John?

'There aren't many people like John in football. In many ways he just doesn't fit in with the "football crowd" because that loyalty, that dedication and that commitment are rare qualities in the game. That meant he stood out, and sometimes people found him hard to get on with because he did stick up for what he believed in, and if you let yourself down you soon knew about it. However, he did a cracking job for me, and both as a player and a coach had an excellent career, and deserves all the recognition he gets for that record because it is incredible really. I can only wish him well because, as I say, there are few people with his values in the game, more's the pity.'

AFTERWORD

I have heard John's view of his career, I have spoken with both his family and those he worked with, now it is time for the biographer, for this is a biography and not an autobiography, despite John's close co-operation, to give his view.

How good was John Trollope as a player? Very good, but not quite absolutely top class is probably the verdict. By his own admission, which is backed up by the likes of Frank Burrows and Don Rogers, John's game relied on fitness, positional awareness and athletic ability. He didn't have, as he would recognise, the tricks that would enable him to easily beat a player one on one. What he did have was the ability, through his speed and tactical nous, to put himself into positions where often there was nobody there to beat. He was very, very good at what he did, and his ability getting forward was second to none.

He could have played in the First Division, of that there is little doubt. There were probably two spells in his career when that could have happened. One was early on in his career. There was a fair amount of press speculation that, as one of the key players in 'Bert's Babes', that he would follow the path to the top flight taken by the likes of Bobby Woodruff, Ernie Hunt and Mike Summerbee. We know that during this period, shortly after getting married in 1965, he had a direct, if illegal, approach from a First Division Club. The fact that he chose not to take the money offered says much about the man.

The second occasion was when he was at the peak of his career as part of the Swindon side of the late 1960s and early 1970s. John would have then been in his mid-20s and had made the adjustment to Second Division football very comfortably. In his own judgement, he was playing the best football of his career, and was revelling playing against better players, game in, game out. He, like others of that team, could have made the step up. However, he chose to stay at Swindon, believing that he could achieve First Division football with his home-town club. By the time it became evident that this was unlikely to happen, he was in his late 20s and was, therefore, less likely to be signed by a top club.

After playing, he found his niche in youth coaching, a job he clearly enjoys even to this day. His spell as manager was ill-advised. With hindsight he should never have taken the job, as not only was it given to him at a time when, unbeknown to the majority of fans, the club had huge financial problems but John's direct and straight-forward style was less suited to dealing with senior players, who often wanted their egos pandering. That is most definitely not John's way of working. He expects people to work hard, have the right attitude and to be committed to club and teammates. Although John had a spell as a player, during the halcyon 1968–1970 era when the dressing room was like that, most football clubs tend not to work that way. As a player John found that difficult, as a manager he found it intolerable.

As a youth-team coach he earned the respect of all those he worked with. He didn't suffer fools, which meant that there would always be some dissent from the youngsters with whom he worked, but it is telling that the majority of players who worked under him felt they gained much from the way he tried to instil the right habits in them, for both football and life. His track record at bringing through youth players to first-team football was good, not exceptional, but this may be more a reflection of the fact that the players he had to work with. It is worth relating that the one real jewel with whom he worked, Paul Rideout, has always been very complimentary of how much he learned from his time with John. The way he was finally treated by the club after 37 years of loyal and successful service was absolutely disgraceful. One can argue the rights and wrongs of Steve McMahon's decision to relieve him of his youth-team duties, a decision which would seem to have been made as much on personality as football grounds, but what is not in doubt is that the board of directors should have intervened and offered him another role in the club. That they didn't reflects badly on them, and the club in general

As a man he is much like he was as a player, really: loyal, committed, hard-working and conscientious. He is an easy man to like, if harder to get to know. He keeps his counsel until he works somebody out. Once he trusts someone he is very open. He is a man of strong views and principles, and he is very prepared to express them and argue his point. It is difficult to argue with Frank Burrows's assessment that John is 'his own man'. It is evidence of someone at ease with themselves that they will stick up for what they think is right and not be swayed by the crowd.

As both a player and a man, he is a worthy holder of The Record.